# CONTENTS

# THE ETHICAL AI BIBLE: A UNIVERSAL GUIDE FOR SAFE AND RESPONSIBLE ARTIFICIAL INTELLIGENCE

By

Tony Yustein © 2024
https://thecode.wiki

# INTRODUCTION: THE FOUNDATION OF ETHICAL AI

* * * * * * * * * * * * * * * * * * * * * * * * * * * * * * * *

*Purpose: Why Humanity Needs an Ethical AI Bible*

In a world increasingly shaped by artificial intelligence, the need for a comprehensive guide to ethical AI development has never been more urgent. As AI technologies advance at an unprecedented pace, they are reshaping industries, redefining societal norms, and influencing decisions that affect millions of lives. This transformative potential, however, comes with profound ethical implications.

Unregulated AI systems have already demonstrated the capacity to:

- **Amplify societal biases**: Discriminatory hiring algorithms, facial recognition systems misidentifying minorities.

- **Manipulate human behavior**: Algorithmic manipulation in social media, influencing elections and fostering misinformation.

- **Cause harm**: Autonomous systems making flawed decisions in critical areas like healthcare and law enforcement.

The world is at a crossroads. Without a unifying framework, AI risks becoming a tool for inequality, exploitation, and harm. An ethical AI Bible is essential to:

1. **Safeguard humanity**: Ensure AI technologies align with human values and rights.

2. **Provide clarity**: Offer actionable guidelines to researchers and policymakers navigating complex ethical dilemmas.

3. **Promote equity**: Prevent AI-driven societal divides by ensuring equal access and unbiased operation.

4. **Foster trust**: Build public confidence in AI by ensuring transparency, accountability, and fairness.

This book serves as the definitive resource for navigating the moral complexities of AI, providing a roadmap to a future where technology serves humanity rather than undermines it.

• • • • • • • • • • • • • • • • • • • • • • • • • • • • • • • • •

*Historical Context: Key Milestones and Ethical Dilemmas in AI Development*

AI's journey from theoretical construct to global disruptor is marked by groundbreaking milestones and sobering ethical lessons.

1. **The Early Foundations (1940s-1950s)**

   – **Milestone**: Alan Turing's conceptualization of machine intelligence and the Turing Test.

   – **Ethical Dilemma**: Early debates over the moral implications of machines mimicking human thought.

2. **The Dawn of AI (1960s-1980s)**

   – **Milestone**: Development of expert systems like DENDRAL and MYCIN in medicine and science.

   – **Ethical Dilemma**: Concerns about replacing human expertise and accountability in critical decisions.

3. **AI Goes Mainstream (1990s-2000s)**

   – **Milestone**: IBM's Deep Blue defeats world chess champion Garry Kasparov, signaling AI's growing capability.

- **Ethical Dilemma**: Public fears about AI surpassing human intelligence and the rise of "black-box" algorithms.

4. **The Data-Driven Revolution (2010s)**

- **Milestone**: Machine learning and neural networks power breakthroughs in language, vision, and decision-making.

- **Ethical Dilemma**: Bias in training data leading to discrimination, from facial recognition to sentencing algorithms.

5. **The Current Era (2020s-Present)**

- **Milestone**: Generative AI systems like ChatGPT and DALL·E reshape creativity, communication, and problem-solving.

- **Ethical Dilemma**: Deepfakes and misinformation threaten public trust, while automation challenges employment paradigms.

Each milestone has been accompanied by ethical questions that society has often struggled to address in real-time. This historical perspective underscores the pressing need for a global, unified standard to guide AI's future development.

• • • • • • • • • • • • • • • • • • • • • • • • • • • • • •

*Target Audience: Researchers, Developers,*
*Policymakers, and Ethicists*

This book is tailored for a diverse audience united by a shared responsibility for ethical AI:

1. **Researchers**:

- Navigating uncharted technical and ethical terrains in AI innovation.

- Ensuring their work upholds the highest standards of

fairness and accountability.

2. **Developers**:

  – Balancing performance with ethical considerations in AI design and implementation.

  – Learning actionable steps to embed ethical principles into every line of code.

3. **Policymakers**:

  – Crafting laws and regulations that protect citizens while fostering innovation.

  – Harmonizing ethical standards across borders for global impact.

4. **Ethicists**:

  – Guiding interdisciplinary discussions on the moral implications of AI.

  – Establishing frameworks that bridge philosophical thought with practical application.

By addressing the unique concerns of these groups, this book becomes an indispensable tool for creating AI systems that serve humanity responsibly and equitably.

• • • • • • • • • • • • • • • • • • • • • • • • • • • • • • • • • • • • • • •

*Vision: Establishing a Global Standard for Ethical AI Development*
The ultimate vision of this book is ambitious yet necessary: to establish a universal ethical framework for AI development that transcends cultural, economic, and political divides. This vision is grounded in three key objectives:

1. **Unity**: Provide a shared ethical language that bridges gaps between nations, industries, and disciplines.

2. **Guidance**: Offer clear, actionable roadmaps for integrating ethics into every stage of AI research, design, deployment, and governance.

3.  **Inspiration**: Foster a global movement of responsible AI innovation, where technology enhances human life rather than endangers it.

This vision is not a static goal but an evolving mission, adapting to the rapidly changing landscape of AI. By providing a comprehensive and actionable guide, this book aspires to empower humanity to harness AI's transformative power responsibly, ethically, and sustainably.

# CHAPTER 1: DEFINING AI ETHICS

● ● ● ● ● ● ● ● ● ● ● ● ● ● ● ● ● ● ● ● ● ● ● ● ● ● ● ● ● ● ● ● ●

*Overview of Ethics in Technology and AI*

Ethics, the study of what is right and wrong, has long been a cornerstone of human society. In the context of technology, ethics focuses on understanding the societal, cultural, and individual impacts of innovation. As technology evolves, its ethical dimensions grow increasingly complex, requiring a dynamic approach to ensure its alignment with human values.

Artificial intelligence (AI) introduces unprecedented ethical considerations. Unlike traditional technologies, AI systems can learn, adapt, and operate autonomously, often making decisions that directly affect human lives. This autonomy amplifies the importance of embedding ethical principles into their development and deployment.

The emergence of ethical challenges in AI mirrors the trajectory of past technologies but introduces unique dimensions:

- The potential for **unintended consequences** due to machine learning algorithms' unpredictability.

- The **scale of impact**, where errors or biases can affect millions in real time.

- The difficulty of assigning **accountability**, given the collaborative and often opaque nature of AI systems.

Understanding and addressing these issues requires grounding in key ethical frameworks tailored to the challenges AI presents.

• • • • • • • • • • • • • • • • • • • • • • • • • • • • • • •

*Key Ethical Frameworks and Their Relevance to AI*

To navigate AI's ethical complexities, three primary ethical frameworks provide guidance: utilitarianism, deontology, and virtue ethics. Each offers a unique lens for evaluating AI's potential benefits and risks.

• • • • • • • • • • • • • • • • • • • • • • • • • • • • • • •

## 1. Utilitarianism: The Ethics of Consequences

- **Definition**: Utilitarianism advocates for actions that maximize overall happiness or utility and minimize harm.

- **Relevance to AI**:

  – AI systems should be designed to deliver the greatest net benefit to society.

  – Example: A healthcare AI prioritizing resource allocation based on potential lives saved.

  – Ethical Dilemma: What happens when maximizing utility benefits the majority but harms vulnerable minorities (e.g., algorithmic bias)?

- **Applications in AI**:

  – Evaluating trade-offs in AI decision-making, such as balancing safety and efficiency in autonomous vehicles.

  – Designing algorithms that optimize societal outcomes while safeguarding against marginalization.

• • • • • • • • • • • • • • • • • • • • • • • • • • • • • • •

## 2. Deontology: The Ethics of Rules and Duties

- **Definition**: Deontology emphasizes adherence to moral rules and duties, regardless of outcomes.

- **Relevance to AI**:

  – AI systems must operate within clearly defined moral boundaries, ensuring they respect fundamental rights and principles.

- Example: An AI system ensuring data privacy, even if sacrificing data could lead to beneficial insights.

- Ethical Dilemma: Strict rule adherence may limit the flexibility needed for certain AI applications (e.g., balancing privacy with public health tracking).

- **Applications in AI**:

  - Ensuring compliance with ethical rules, such as never using AI to propagate misinformation.

  - Embedding fail-safes to prevent rule violations, regardless of potential utility.

• • • • • • • • • • • • • • • • • • • • • • • • • • • • • • • • • • •

## 3. Virtue Ethics: The Ethics of Character

- **Definition**: Virtue ethics focuses on cultivating moral character and virtues such as honesty, fairness, and compassion.

- **Relevance to AI**:

  - Developers and organizations must embody ethical virtues in their work, ensuring AI reflects these values.

  - Example: An AI chatbot designed to engage with empathy and respect, avoiding manipulative behavior.

  - Ethical Dilemma: Virtues can be subjective and context-dependent, making standardization challenging.

- **Applications in AI**:

  - Encouraging developers to adopt ethical codes of conduct.

  - Designing AI to model and promote virtuous behavior in user interactions.

• • • • • • • • • • • • • • • • • • • • • • • • • • • • • • • • • • •

*Unique Challenges of AI Ethics Compared to Traditional Systems*

AI ethics goes beyond traditional technology ethics in several critical ways:

1. **Autonomy and Decision-Making**:

   – Traditional systems follow pre-programmed instructions.

   – AI can make decisions independently, raising questions of accountability and unpredictability.

2. **Scale and Speed**:

   – AI operates on a massive scale, often in real time, magnifying the consequences of ethical lapses.

3. **Opacity**:

   – Many AI systems are "black boxes," where decision-making processes are not easily explainable, complicating accountability.

4. **Bias Amplification**:

   – Unlike static technologies, AI systems can learn and perpetuate biases, exacerbating systemic inequalities.

5. **Dynamic Evolution**:

   – AI systems evolve with use, meaning their ethical behavior can change over time, requiring continuous oversight.

Addressing these challenges necessitates integrating ethical considerations at every stage of AI development, from conception to deployment.

• • • • • • • • • • • • • • • • • • • • • • • • • • • • • • • • • •

*Checklist for AI Ethics Integration*

To ensure that ethical principles guide AI development, teams should follow these steps:

1. **Familiarize the Team with Core Ethical Frameworks**:

   – Conduct workshops or training sessions on utilitarianism, deontology, and virtue ethics.

–   Provide case studies demonstrating the application of these frameworks in AI scenarios.

2. **Discuss Ethical Priorities for the AI System Under Development**:

–   Identify the primary ethical concerns relevant to the AI system (e.g., fairness, transparency, privacy).

–   Document decisions made about trade-offs between competing ethical principles (e.g., utility vs. privacy).

–   Assign team members responsibility for monitoring ethical compliance during development.

By embedding these practices into the team's workflow, ethical considerations become an integral part of the AI development lifecycle.

• • • • • • • • • • • • • • • • • • • • • • • • • • • • • • • • • • • • •

# CHAPTER 2:
# THE UNIVERSAL
# PRINCIPLES OF
# ETHICAL AI

As artificial intelligence becomes increasingly integrated into society, a set of universal principles must guide its development and deployment. These principles —**Transparency**, **Accountability**, **Fairness**, **Safety**, and **Sustainability**—ensure that AI systems align with human values and serve as tools for equitable and responsible progress. This chapter explores each principle in detail, illustrating their significance, challenges, and practical application.

*Transparency: Making AI Systems Understandable*

Transparency ensures that AI systems are explainable, accessible, and understandable to users, developers, and regulators. It addresses the inherent complexity of AI models, particularly those utilizing machine learning or deep learning, where decisions may be difficult to trace.

1. **Why Transparency Matters**:

   – Builds trust among users by demystifying AI decision-making.

   – Facilitates accountability by making it clear how and

why decisions were made.

–    Helps identify and mitigate biases or errors in AI processes.

2. **Challenges to Transparency**:

–    Complex "black-box" models, where the logic behind decisions is difficult to explain.

–    Trade-offs between explainability and performance in high-accuracy systems.

3. **Practical Steps for Achieving Transparency**:

–    Develop interpretable models that provide clear explanations of their decisions.

–    Use visualization tools to illustrate AI processes and outcomes.

–    Provide documentation that is accessible to both technical and non-technical stakeholders.

• • • • • • • • • • • • • • • • • • • • • • • • • • • • • • • • • • • • • •

*Accountability: Who Is Responsible When AI Goes Wrong*

Accountability ensures that individuals or organizations can be held responsible for AI systems' decisions and outcomes. It addresses the diffusion of responsibility in complex AI ecosystems.

1. **Why Accountability Matters**:

–    Protects users and society from harm by providing clear channels for redress.

–    Encourages ethical behavior among developers and organizations.

–    Prevents the use of AI as a scapegoat for unethical or harmful decisions.

2. **Challenges to Accountability**:

- Shared responsibilities among developers, vendors, and users can blur lines of accountability.

- Autonomous decision-making complicates the assignment of blame.

3. **Practical Steps for Ensuring Accountability**:

- Assign clear roles and responsibilities throughout the AI lifecycle.

- Establish governance frameworks with mechanisms for auditing and compliance.

- Implement logging and traceability features to track decisions and identify potential failures.

• • • • • • • • • • • • • • • • • • • • • • • • • • • • • • • • •

*Fairness: Ensuring Equity Across Demographics*

Fairness ensures that AI systems operate without discrimination, providing equitable outcomes for all individuals and groups. It mitigates the risk of perpetuating or amplifying societal biases.

1. **Why Fairness Matters**:

- Promotes equality and justice in AI applications.

- Protects vulnerable populations from systemic biases.

- Enhances trust and acceptance of AI systems.

2. **Challenges to Fairness**:

- Bias in training data reflecting historical inequities.

- Cultural and contextual differences complicating the definition of fairness.

3. **Practical Steps for Achieving Fairness**:

- Use diverse datasets to train AI models, representing all relevant demographics.

- Regularly audit systems for bias using fairness-testing

tools.

–   Engage diverse stakeholders to assess fairness in real-world contexts.

• • • • • • • • • • • • • • • • • • • • • • • • • • • • • • • •

*Safety: Designing Systems for Secure and Reliable Operation*
Safety ensures that AI systems function reliably under diverse conditions and are protected from misuse or malicious attacks. It encompasses both physical and digital safety.

1. **Why Safety Matters:**

–   Prevents harm caused by system errors or failures.

–   Protects sensitive data and infrastructure from cybersecurity threats.

–   Ensures AI systems adapt responsibly to unexpected scenarios.

2. **Challenges to Safety:**

–   Unpredictable behavior in machine learning systems when exposed to novel inputs.

–   Vulnerabilities to hacking or adversarial attacks.

3. **Practical Steps for Ensuring Safety:**

–   Conduct rigorous testing under extreme and edge-case conditions.

–   Develop fail-safe mechanisms and emergency shutdown protocols.

–   Regularly update systems to address emerging vulnerabilities.

• • • • • • • • • • • • • • • • • • • • • • • • • • • • • • • •

*Sustainability: Minimizing Environmental Impact*
Sustainability emphasizes reducing the environmental footprint of AI development and operation. AI systems,

particularly those requiring substantial computational resources, can significantly impact energy consumption and ecological balance.

1. **Why Sustainability Matters**:

– Addresses the increasing energy demands of large-scale AI models.

– Aligns AI development with global environmental goals.

– Ensures long-term viability of AI technologies.

2. **Challenges to Sustainability**:

– High energy consumption during training and inference of large models.

– Trade-offs between efficiency and performance.

3. **Practical Steps for Ensuring Sustainability**:

– Optimize algorithms and infrastructure for energy efficiency.

– Use renewable energy sources for AI operations.

– Monitor and report the carbon footprint of AI projects.

• • • • • • • • • • • • • • • • • • • • • • • • • • • • • • • • •

*Checklist: Integrating the Principles of Ethical AI*
To ensure these principles are embedded in the AI system, teams should follow these steps:

1. **Document Integration of Each Principle**:

– Record how transparency, accountability, fairness, safety, and sustainability are addressed during the design, testing, and deployment phases.

– Include these details in technical documentation for internal and external audits.

2. **Perform Principle-Alignment Reviews**:

–    Conduct regular reviews to assess compliance with ethical principles at every stage of development.

–    Use diverse review teams, including ethicists and end-users, to provide comprehensive feedback.

–    Update the system and processes as necessary to address gaps or evolving standards.

. . . . . . . . . . . . . . . . . . . . . . . . . . . . . . . . . . . .

By embedding these principles into the development and deployment lifecycle, AI systems can align with societal values, fostering trust, reliability, and equity. These universal principles serve as a foundation for ethical AI, ensuring its responsible integration into the fabric of human life.

. . . . . . . . . . . . . . . . . . . . . . . . . . . . . . . . . . . .

# CHAPTER 3: HUMAN RIGHTS AND AI

• • • • • • • • • • • • • • • • • • • • • • • • • • • • • • • •

*Introduction*

Artificial intelligence (AI) is reshaping the modern world, influencing areas such as healthcare, education, law enforcement, and entertainment. While its potential to enhance human rights is immense, so are the risks of violating them. This chapter explores how AI impacts universal human rights, the legal implications of these impacts, and real-world case studies highlighting successes and failures in protecting these rights.

• • • • • • • • • • • • • • • • • • • • • • • • • • • • • • • •

*Mapping AI's Impact on Universal Human Rights*

Human rights, as defined by the **Universal Declaration of Human Rights (UDHR)**, include the rights to equality, privacy, freedom of expression, and more. AI systems have profound implications for these rights, both positive and negative.

1. **Positive Impacts**:

   – **Equality**: AI can reduce discrimination by identifying and correcting systemic biases (e.g., fairer hiring algorithms, unbiased credit scoring systems).

   – **Access to Justice**: AI-powered tools like legal chatbots and predictive analytics enhance access to legal resources for underserved populations.

   – **Healthcare**: AI-driven diagnostics and resource

allocation improve access to life-saving treatments in remote or underprivileged areas.

2. **Negative Impacts:**

– **Right to Privacy:**

- Mass surveillance systems often violate individual privacy, as seen in widespread data harvesting by tech companies.

– **Freedom of Expression:**

- Content moderation algorithms may suppress dissent or limit free speech by over-blocking legitimate discussions.

– **Non-Discrimination:**

- Biased AI systems perpetuate racial, gender, or socioeconomic inequities (e.g., biased hiring systems, facial recognition failures targeting minorities).

3. **Emerging Concerns:**

– The right to **digital autonomy**, as AI systems increasingly influence decision-making in personal, financial, and social contexts.

– The right to **algorithmic transparency**, ensuring users understand how AI decisions are made.

• • • • • • • • • • • • • • • • • • • • • • • • • • • • • • • • • • • • •

*Legal Implications of Rights Violations Through AI*

The intersection of AI and human rights poses significant legal challenges. Many existing legal frameworks struggle to address the nuances of AI-related rights violations.

1. **Global Legal Frameworks:**

– **Universal Declaration of Human Rights (UDHR):** A foundational document applicable to AI's impact on global rights.

– **General Data Protection Regulation (GDPR)**: EU legislation emphasizing data protection and privacy, with specific provisions addressing automated decision-making.

– **Convention on Human Rights (ECHR)**: Enforces the right to privacy and fair treatment, increasingly relevant in AI-related cases.

2. **Key Legal Issues**:

– **Accountability**: Determining liability in cases of AI-driven rights violations.

  • Example: Who is responsible when a facial recognition system leads to wrongful arrests?

– **Lack of Regulation**:

  • Inconsistent global standards create loopholes for unethical AI deployment.

– **Algorithmic Bias and Discrimination**:

  • Legal consequences for organizations deploying biased systems that harm protected groups.

3. **Advancements in Legal Standards**:

– Proposed AI-specific regulations, such as the EU's **Artificial Intelligence Act**, aim to classify and regulate high-risk AI applications.

– Increasing calls for international agreements to establish global AI ethics and rights-protection frameworks.

• • • • • • • • • • • • • • • • • • • • • • • • • • • • • •

*Case Studies of AI Systems That Infringed or Protected Rights*
1. **Case Study: AI Infringing Rights**

- **Example**: Facial Recognition in Law Enforcement

  - **Problem**: Several studies have shown that facial recognition algorithms are significantly less accurate in identifying women and people of color. These inaccuracies have led to wrongful arrests and detentions, violating the rights to equality and due process.

  - **Impact**: Discrimination and loss of trust in law enforcement.

  - **Resolution Efforts**: Some jurisdictions, like San Francisco, have banned the use of facial recognition technology by government agencies.

2. **Case Study: AI Protecting Rights**

- **Example**: AI in Disaster Relief

  - **Positive Impact**: AI systems have been used to predict natural disasters, allocate resources, and identify survivors in real-time. For example, during Hurricane Harvey, AI tools helped locate stranded individuals through social media data.

  - **Human Rights Enhanced**: The right to life and safety.

3. **Case Study: Mixed Outcomes**

- **Example**: Content Moderation on Social Media

  - **Positive Impact**: AI tools detect and remove harmful content, protecting users from online abuse.

  - **Negative Impact**: Over-moderation has suppressed legitimate discussions, violating the right to free expression.

• • • • • • • • • • • • • • • • • • • • • • • • • • • • • • • • • • • • • •

*Practical Framework for AI and Human Rights*

To balance innovation and protection, organizations must adopt a proactive approach to safeguarding human rights.

1. **Rights-Impact Assessments**:

   – Assess potential risks to human rights at every stage of AI development.

   – Consider direct impacts (e.g., privacy) and indirect consequences (e.g., systemic biases).

   – Use human rights impact assessment tools aligned with international frameworks.

2. **Safeguards for User Rights**:

   – Embed privacy-by-design principles into AI systems.

   – Regularly audit AI systems for compliance with legal and ethical standards.

   – Establish user grievance mechanisms for addressing rights violations.

3. **Advocacy and Collaboration**:

   – Collaborate with regulators, ethicists, and human rights organizations to refine AI systems.

   – Advocate for stronger global standards protecting human rights in AI.

• • • • • • • • • • • • • • • • • • • • • • • • • • • • • • • • • • • •

*Checklist: Protecting Human Rights in AI Development*

1. **Conduct a Rights-Impact Assessment**:

   – Identify human rights that the AI system may affect (positively and negatively).

   – Map risks across the lifecycle of the AI system, from design to deployment.

   – Document findings and mitigation strategies.

2.  **Establish Safeguards for Protecting User Rights**:

–   Implement privacy-by-design principles and ensure data is handled ethically.

–   Regularly test AI for bias and fairness.

–   Provide transparent documentation for users and regulators.

–   Create accessible grievance mechanisms for users to report potential rights violations.

• • • • • • • • • • • • • • • • • • • • • • • • • • • • • • • • • •

*Conclusion*

AI has the potential to be a transformative force for protecting and enhancing human rights, but it also poses significant risks of violation. Through proactive assessments, legal compliance, and robust safeguards, developers and policymakers can ensure AI serves as a tool for equity and justice. This chapter underscores the necessity of embedding human rights considerations into every stage of AI development, paving the way for a future where technology upholds and amplifies humanity's most fundamental values.

• • • • • • • • • • • • • • • • • • • • • • • • • • • • • • • •

# CHAPTER 4:
# ETHICAL DILEMMAS
# AND CONFLICT
# RESOLUTION IN AI

• • • • • • • • • • • • • • • • • • • • • • • • • • • • • • • • •

*Introduction*

The integration of artificial intelligence (AI) into critical sectors—healthcare, finance, law enforcement, and more—has introduced complex ethical dilemmas. These conflicts arise from competing values and priorities, such as balancing individual privacy against societal utility or optimizing performance while ensuring fairness. Addressing these challenges requires systematic frameworks and practical training to navigate the intricate ethical terrain of AI development and deployment.

This chapter explores common ethical dilemmas in AI, provides actionable frameworks for resolving value conflicts, and introduces scenario-based training to prepare teams for real-world ethical decision-making.

• • • • • • • • • • • • • • • • • • • • • • • • • • • • • • • • •

*Common Ethical Dilemmas in AI*

Ethical dilemmas occur when there is no clear right or wrong answer but rather a trade-off between competing priorities. Below are some of the most pressing ethical conflicts in AI:

1. **Privacy vs. Utility**:

–       **Example**: AI in healthcare may require extensive patient data to optimize diagnoses and treatments. However, collecting and processing such data can infringe on individuals' privacy.

–    **Key Questions**:

  •        How can the system maximize public health benefits without compromising individual privacy?

  •       Are there mechanisms to anonymize data while retaining its utility?

2.   **Transparency vs. Performance**:

–       **Example**: Complex deep learning models often achieve high accuracy but are opaque ("black-box models"). Simpler, interpretable models may sacrifice some performance.

–    **Key Questions**:

  •       Is it acceptable to prioritize performance over explainability in high-stakes contexts?

  •       How can developers ensure accountability in opaque systems?

3.   **Autonomy vs. Oversight**:

–       **Example**: Autonomous vehicles must make split-second decisions that can involve life-or-death trade-offs, such as choosing between hitting pedestrians or risking passenger safety.

–    **Key Questions**:

  •       Should AI systems have the authority to act independently in such scenarios?

  •       How can human oversight be balanced with the need for real-time decision-making?

4. **Fairness vs. Efficiency:**

   – **Example**: AI algorithms used in hiring may prioritize efficiency and cost-saving, potentially overlooking qualified candidates from underrepresented groups.

   – **Key Questions**:

      • How can fairness metrics be integrated without compromising efficiency?

      • Is the cost of additional fairness mechanisms justified?

5. **Innovation vs. Regulation:**

   – **Example**: Developers often face pressure to innovate rapidly, sometimes at the expense of ethical compliance.

   – **Key Questions**:

      • How can regulatory oversight encourage innovation without stifling it?

      • What safeguards ensure ethical innovation under tight deadlines?

• • • • • • • • • • • • • • • • • • • • • • • • • • • • • • • • • • • • • • •

*Frameworks for Resolving Conflicts in Ethical Values*
To address these dilemmas systematically, AI teams can adopt structured frameworks that balance competing ethical priorities. Below are three widely applicable frameworks:

1. **The Ethical Matrix:**

   – **Description**: A grid-based tool that evaluates the impact of decisions across multiple stakeholders and ethical principles.

   – **Steps**:

      • List stakeholders (e.g., users, organizations, regulators).

- Identify relevant ethical principles (e.g., fairness, privacy, utility).

- Evaluate the impact of each decision on all stakeholders and principles.

– **Use Case**: Choosing between performance and transparency in AI model design.

2. **The Trolley Problem Adaptation for AI**:

– **Description**: A scenario-based approach to examining trade-offs in high-stakes decisions, inspired by the classic ethical dilemma.

– **Steps**:

- Define the dilemma (e.g., prioritizing safety of pedestrians vs. passengers in autonomous vehicles).

- Simulate outcomes of various decision paths.

- Apply ethical principles to justify the chosen path.

– **Use Case**: Autonomous systems making real-time decisions with moral implications.

3. **The Stakeholder-Engaged Process**:

– **Description**: Involves actively engaging diverse stakeholders to balance ethical priorities.

– **Steps**:

- Gather input from impacted stakeholders.

- Create consensus-driven solutions to resolve ethical conflicts.

- Reassess solutions as the system evolves.

– **Use Case**: Designing hiring algorithms that balance fairness and efficiency.

• • • • • • • • • • • • • • • • • • • • • • • • • • • • • • • • • •

## *Scenario-Based Training for Ethical Decision-Making*

Scenario-based training is a powerful tool for equipping AI teams with the skills to navigate ethical dilemmas. These exercises simulate real-world conflicts, encouraging teams to apply frameworks and principles in practice.

1. **Example Scenario 1: Privacy vs. Public Health**:

   – **Scenario**: A government wants to deploy an AI-powered pandemic tracking app that collects real-time location data from users. While the app can save lives, it raises privacy concerns.

   – **Task**:

     • Debate the ethical trade-offs between individual privacy and public health benefits.

     • Develop a plan to anonymize data while retaining its utility.

2. **Example Scenario 2: Fairness in Hiring**:

   – **Scenario**: An AI hiring tool disproportionately favors male candidates for engineering roles. Adjusting the algorithm reduces bias but lowers efficiency.

   – **Task**:

     • Propose ways to improve fairness without significantly compromising efficiency.

     • Justify the trade-offs to organizational stakeholders.

3. **Example Scenario 3: Autonomous Vehicles**:

   – **Scenario**: An autonomous car must decide whether to swerve and risk the passenger's safety or stay on course and risk hitting pedestrians.

   – **Task**:

- Apply the Trolley Problem framework to justify the car's programming.

- Discuss the role of human oversight in such scenarios.

• • • • • • • • • • • • • • • • • • • • • • • • • • • • • • • •

*Checklist: Ethical Dilemmas and Conflict Resolution*

1. **Identify and Document Ethical Dilemmas Early in the Design Phase**:

   – Conduct brainstorming sessions to anticipate ethical conflicts.

   – Record all potential dilemmas and their likely impacts on stakeholders.

2. **Develop a Decision-Making Framework for Conflicting Scenarios**:

   – Select an appropriate framework (e.g., Ethical Matrix, Trolley Problem Adaptation, Stakeholder-Engaged Process).

   – Ensure the framework is integrated into the project workflow.

   – Test the framework using scenario-based exercises to refine decision-making.

• • • • • • • • • • • • • • • • • • • • • • • • • • • • • • • •

*Conclusion*

Ethical dilemmas in AI are inevitable but manageable with the right tools and approaches. By identifying and addressing conflicts early, using structured frameworks, and training teams with real-world scenarios, organizations can ensure that their AI systems reflect ethical integrity. This chapter provides a practical guide to navigating the complex trade-offs inherent in AI development, paving the way for responsible and equitable technology.

# CHAPTER 5:
# DESIGNING ETHICAL
# AI SYSTEMS

• • • • • • • • • • • • • • • • • • • • • • • • • • • • • • • •

*Introduction*

Designing ethical AI systems is not just about solving technical problems; it is about embedding ethical principles into the architecture, processes, and goals of the system. This requires deliberate actions to ensure that ethical considerations are prioritized from the earliest stages of development. By integrating interdisciplinary expertise and building adaptive systems, organizations can create AI solutions that evolve with societal needs and values.

This chapter explores how to embed ethics into AI architecture, the importance of interdisciplinary collaboration, and methods for creating systems capable of adapting to changing ethical standards.

• • • • • • • • • • • • • • • • • • • • • • • • • • • • • • • •

*Embedding Ethical Principles into AI Architecture*

Ethical principles such as transparency, fairness, accountability, and safety must be foundational elements of an AI system's architecture. Here's how these principles can be embedded:

1. **Transparency by Design**:

   – **Approach**: Create systems where decision-making processes can be easily explained.

   –   **Implementation**:

- Design interpretable models, such as decision trees or rule-based systems, where applicable.

- Use tools like SHAP (SHapley Additive exPlanations) or LIME (Local Interpretable Model-Agnostic Explanations) for explainability in complex models.

- Incorporate clear documentation detailing system logic and decision pathways.

2. **Fairness in Algorithms**:

–   **Approach**: Ensure algorithms do not perpetuate or amplify biases.

–   **Implementation**:

- Use fairness metrics (e.g., demographic parity, equal opportunity).

- Train models on diverse datasets that represent all demographics fairly.

- Regularly audit for unintended biases.

3. **Accountability Mechanisms**:

–   **Approach**: Assign responsibility for system behavior and decisions.

–   **Implementation**:

- Embed logging features to track decision-making processes.

- Design fallback systems allowing for human intervention when needed.

- Establish clear documentation of roles and responsibilities.

4. **Safety and Security**:

- **Approach**: Mitigate risks by designing systems that prioritize reliability and resilience.

- **Implementation**:

  - Conduct extensive testing for edge cases and adversarial scenarios.

  - Develop robust error-handling and fail-safe protocols.

  - Regularly update systems to address vulnerabilities.

• • • • • • • • • • • • • • • • • • • • • • • • • • • • • • • • • •

*Creating Interdisciplinary Teams with Ethicists and Sociologists*

Ethical AI design requires collaboration beyond technical experts. Involving ethicists, sociologists, and other non-technical stakeholders ensures diverse perspectives are considered.

1. **The Role of Interdisciplinary Teams**:

- **Ethicists**: Identify and address potential ethical dilemmas during development.

- **Sociologists**: Analyze societal implications and potential biases.

- **Legal Experts**: Ensure compliance with relevant laws and regulations.

- **End-Users**: Provide insights into real-world impacts and usability.

2. **Fostering Collaboration**:

- Host regular cross-disciplinary meetings to align goals and expectations.

- Encourage open dialogue to identify potential blind spots.

- Integrate ethical considerations into the development

process as milestones.

3. **Practical Steps for Building Interdisciplinary Teams**:

– Recruit experts from diverse academic and professional backgrounds.

– Train non-technical stakeholders on AI basics to enable meaningful contributions.

– Involve external consultants for specialized issues (e.g., data privacy).

• • • • • • • • • • • • • • • • • • • • • • • • • • • • • • • • • • •

*Building Systems That Adapt to Evolving Ethical Standards*
AI systems operate in dynamic environments where ethical norms and societal expectations may shift. Designing adaptive systems ensures long-term compliance with emerging standards.

1. **Incorporating Adaptive Features**:

– Implement feedback loops to monitor system performance and ethical compliance.

– Use machine learning models that can retrain on updated datasets reflecting new standards.

– Develop modular architectures that allow for iterative improvements.

2. **Continuous Ethical Auditing**:

– Conduct regular assessments of the system's impact on stakeholders.

– Use AI ethics toolkits, such as IBM's AI Fairness 360 or Microsoft's Fairlearn, to evaluate compliance.

– Update ethical guidelines and integrate them into future development cycles.

3. **Scenario Planning**:

- Anticipate potential ethical challenges in evolving scenarios (e.g., new laws, cultural shifts).

- Develop contingency plans to address these challenges proactively.

• • • • • • • • • • • • • • • • • • • • • • • • • • • • • •

*Checklist: Ethical Design Practices*

1. **Host Ethical Design Workshops During Early Stages:**

- Organize brainstorming sessions with interdisciplinary teams to identify potential ethical challenges.

- Use structured tools like ethical matrices or value-sensitive design frameworks.

- Document insights and integrate them into the design blueprint.

2. **Include Diverse Perspectives in the Development Team:**

- Recruit individuals from varied demographic, cultural, and professional backgrounds.

- Actively engage non-technical stakeholders to ensure holistic system evaluation.

- Establish a feedback mechanism for ongoing input during development.

3. **Integrate Ethical Testing Protocols:**

- Define ethical benchmarks (e.g., fairness thresholds, transparency metrics).

- Use scenario-based testing to simulate real-world impacts.

- Audit results regularly and adjust designs as needed.

4. **Build a Governance Framework:**

–  Assign roles for ethical oversight, including an ethics officer or committee.

–  Develop policies for handling ethical breaches or violations.

–  Establish transparent reporting mechanisms for internal and external stakeholders.

• • • • • • • • • • • • • • • • • • • • • • • • • • • • • • • • •

*Conclusion*

Designing ethical AI systems requires more than technical excellence; it demands a commitment to embedding ethical principles, fostering interdisciplinary collaboration, and preparing for evolving standards. By integrating these practices into the development lifecycle, organizations can ensure their AI systems are not only innovative but also responsible, fair, and aligned with human values.

This chapter provides a roadmap for designing AI systems that uphold the highest ethical standards, empowering teams to build solutions that truly benefit society.

• • • • • • • • • • • • • • • • • • • • • • • • • • • • • • • •

# CHAPTER 6: DATA ETHICS IN AI

*Introduction*

Data is the lifeblood of artificial intelligence, shaping its decisions, predictions, and actions. However, the ethical use of data in AI presents significant challenges, including concerns about consent, transparency, bias, and the handling of sensitive information. This chapter explores the principles of ethical data collection and management, techniques for preventing bias, and strategies for handling sensitive or restricted data. By adhering to these practices, AI developers can build systems that respect user rights, ensure fairness, and align with legal and societal expectations.

*Principles of Ethical Data Collection*

Ethical data collection is foundational to trustworthy AI systems. It ensures that data acquisition respects individuals' rights while providing accurate, reliable inputs for AI models. Key principles include:

1. **Consent**:

   – **Definition**: Data collection must be conducted with the informed, voluntary consent of individuals.

   – **Implementation**:

     • Use clear, understandable language when seeking consent.

- Specify the purpose of data collection, how it will be used, and for how long.

- Provide users with the ability to withdraw consent at any time.

- **Examples**:

    - Consent forms for app users specifying data-sharing terms.

    - Opt-in mechanisms for cookies and tracking tools on websites.

2. **Transparency**:

- **Definition**: Users should know what data is being collected, how it will be used, and who will have access to it.

- **Implementation**:

    - Publish privacy policies and data-handling practices.

    - Use visualizations or dashboards to show users how their data is processed.

    - Notify users promptly about changes in data use policies.

- **Examples**:

    - Social media platforms showing users which ads are targeted based on their data.

    - Open data platforms explaining the source and scope of shared datasets.

3. **Anonymization**:

- **Definition**: Personal identifiers are removed or obscured to prevent linking data back to individuals.

- **Implementation**:

- Apply techniques like pseudonymization, aggregation, or differential privacy.

- Regularly review and update anonymization methods to address emerging risks.

- **Examples**:

  - Anonymizing patient records in medical research to ensure privacy.

  - Aggregating location data for urban planning without revealing individual movements.

• • • • • • • • • • • • • • • • • • • • • • • • • • • • • • • • • • •

*Preventing Bias in Datasets*

Bias in datasets can perpetuate and even amplify inequalities in AI systems. Addressing bias is critical to ensure fairness and equity.

1. **Sources of Bias**:

   - **Historical Bias**: Data reflecting past inequalities (e.g., gender pay gaps).

   - **Sampling Bias**: Overrepresentation or underrepresentation of certain groups.

   - **Labeling Bias**: Human errors or subjective judgments in labeling data.

2. **Techniques to Prevent and Mitigate Bias**:

   - **Diverse Data Sources**:

     - Collect data from multiple sources to represent all demographics fairly.

     - Ensure geographic, cultural, and socioeconomic diversity in datasets.

   - **Bias Audits**:

     - Regularly evaluate datasets using fairness metrics

(e.g., disparate impact ratio).

- Identify and correct skewed distributions.

    – **Algorithmic Adjustments**:

- Use techniques like reweighting or resampling to balance datasets.

- Train models to be invariant to sensitive attributes (e.g., race, gender).

3. **Real-World Example**:

    – A hiring algorithm trained on biased historical data perpetuated gender discrimination by favoring male candidates. By auditing and retraining the model on a balanced dataset, fairness was improved.

· · · · · · · · · · · · · · · · · · · · · · · · · · · · · · · · ·

*Handling Sensitive or Restricted Data*

Sensitive data requires extra precautions to protect individuals' rights and comply with regulations.

1. **Defining Sensitive Data**:

    – Personal identifiers (e.g., names, Social Security numbers).

    – Health data, financial records, and biometric information.

    – Data subject to legal restrictions (e.g., GDPR, HIPAA).

2. **Best Practices for Handling Sensitive Data**:

    – **Access Control**:

- Restrict access to sensitive data to authorized personnel only.

- Use role-based access controls (RBAC) to limit unnecessary exposure.

    – **Data Encryption**:

- Encrypt sensitive data during storage and transmission.
- Regularly update encryption protocols to address evolving threats.

- **Data Minimization**:
  - Collect only the data necessary for the intended purpose.
  - Delete unused or redundant data promptly.

- **Compliance Monitoring**:
  - Regularly review processes to ensure adherence to legal and ethical standards.
  - Conduct third-party audits for unbiased evaluations.

3. **Real-World Example**:

- A healthcare provider implemented robust encryption and anonymization for patient data used in an AI diagnostic tool, ensuring compliance with HIPAA and protecting user privacy.

• • • • • • • • • • • • • • • • • • • • • • • • • • • • • • • •

*Checklist: Ethical Data Practices*

1. **Verify Dataset Compliance with Privacy Laws**:

- Ensure datasets adhere to laws like GDPR, CCPA, HIPAA, or local regulations.
- Maintain a clear record of data sources, collection methods, and legal permissions.

2. **Analyze Datasets for Bias and Correct Imbalances**:

- Use fairness metrics to identify underrepresentation or overrepresentation of groups.
- Apply balancing techniques (e.g., oversampling,

synthetic data generation).

– Conduct regular audits to evaluate and mitigate potential biases.

3. **Document Data-Handling Processes**:

– Create a detailed data lineage report, tracking the flow of data from collection to usage.

– Record anonymization and encryption techniques used to protect sensitive information.

– Publish data-handling policies and ensure transparency with stakeholders.

• • • • • • • • • • • • • • • • • • • • • • • • • • • • • • • • •

*Conclusion*

Data ethics is the cornerstone of responsible AI development. By adhering to principles of consent, transparency, and anonymization, preventing bias, and implementing robust safeguards for sensitive data, AI developers can ensure their systems respect individual rights and promote fairness. This chapter provides the foundation for ethical data practices, enabling organizations to build trust, comply with legal requirements, and deliver equitable AI solutions.

• • • • • • • • • • • • • • • • • • • • • • • • • • • • • • • • •

# CHAPTER 7: RIGOROUS TESTING FOR ETHICAL AI

. . . . . . . . . . . . . . . . . . . . . . . . . . . . . . . .

## *Introduction*

Rigorous testing is fundamental to ensuring that AI systems operate ethically, reliably, and safely. It serves as the critical phase where potential biases, risks, and vulnerabilities are identified and mitigated before deployment. Ethical testing not only validates the system's alignment with core principles but also safeguards against harmful consequences in real-world applications.

This chapter outlines methods for testing bias, fairness, and safety, stress-testing AI systems for worst-case scenarios, and designing fail-safes, kill switches, and self-monitoring mechanisms. By implementing these strategies, organizations can ensure that their AI systems uphold ethical and operational standards.

. . . . . . . . . . . . . . . . . . . . . . . . . . . . . . . .

## *Testing for Bias, Fairness, and Safety*

AI systems must be rigorously evaluated for bias, fairness, and safety to minimize harm and ensure equitable outcomes.

1. **Bias Testing**:

   – **Objective**: Identify and mitigate biases that may lead to discriminatory outcomes.

- **Techniques**:

  - Use fairness metrics, such as disparate impact ratio, equality of opportunity, and demographic parity.

  - Evaluate model outputs across demographic groups to detect skewed results.

  - Use debiasing techniques, such as reweighting training samples or adversarial debiasing.

- **Example**: A loan approval AI system must be tested to ensure it does not unfairly reject applications from minority groups.

2. **Fairness Testing**:

- **Objective**: Ensure equitable treatment and representation across all user groups.

- **Techniques**:

  - Test for fairness across multiple axes (e.g., age, gender, ethnicity).

  - Simulate real-world scenarios to evaluate equitable outcomes.

- **Example**: A healthcare diagnostic tool must provide consistent accuracy across different patient demographics.

3. **Safety Testing**:

- **Objective**: Verify that the system operates reliably under diverse conditions and prevents unintended consequences.

- **Techniques**:

  - Test for system robustness using adversarial inputs.

- • Evaluate fail-safe responses in simulated failure scenarios.

- – **Example**: An autonomous vehicle must be tested to handle unexpected obstacles safely.

• • • • • • • • • • • • • • • • • • • • • • • • • • • • • • •

*Stress-Testing AI Systems for Worst-Case Scenarios*
Stress-testing evaluates the system's performance under extreme conditions, identifying vulnerabilities that may not surface during normal operation.

1. **Purpose**:

- – Assess system reliability and stability under high loads or adverse conditions.

- – Ensure robustness against intentional or unintentional misuse.

2. **Methods**:

- – **Extreme Data Inputs**: Test the system with out-of-distribution or adversarial data to identify weaknesses.

  - • Example: Inputting gibberish or contradictory data to a chatbot to observe its behavior.

- – **High-Load Testing**: Simulate peak usage scenarios to evaluate system stability.

  - • Example: Testing an AI-powered customer service system under extreme traffic conditions.

- – **Failure Simulation**: Introduce faults or errors to evaluate the system's recovery mechanisms.

  - • Example: Simulating sensor failures in an autonomous vehicle.

3. **Case Study**:

- – **Example**: A financial AI system underwent stress-testing to ensure stability during market crashes. This included simulating extreme volatility and observing its decision-making patterns under stress.

. . . . . . . . . . . . . . . . . . . . . . . . . . . . . . . . . .

*Designing Fail-Safes, Kill Switches, and Self-Monitoring Mechanisms*

Fail-safes and emergency controls are essential for mitigating harm when an AI system behaves unpredictably or malfunctions.

1. **Fail-Safes**:

    – **Definition**: Built-in mechanisms that allow the system to revert to a safe state during errors.

    – **Implementation**:

        • Use redundancy systems to maintain functionality if critical components fail.

        • Program fallback protocols for high-stakes scenarios.

    – **Example**: A robotic arm halts operation if sensors detect unsafe conditions.

2. **Kill Switches**:

    – **Definition**: Mechanisms for immediate shutdown in emergencies.

    – **Implementation**:

        • Ensure kill switches are easily accessible to authorized personnel.

        • Integrate automatic shutdown protocols for specific triggers (e.g., overheating, security breach).

    – **Example**: A medical AI system has a kill switch to cease operations if it generates anomalous outputs.

3. **Self-Monitoring Mechanisms**:

- **Definition**: Systems that continuously monitor their own performance and detect anomalies.
- **Implementation**:
  - Use real-time diagnostics to evaluate system behavior.
  - Implement anomaly detection algorithms to flag unusual patterns.
- **Example**: An AI-powered factory robot monitors its performance and alerts supervisors to potential mechanical failures.

• • • • • • • • • • • • • • • • • • • • • • • • • • • • • • • • • •

*Checklist: Ensuring Rigorous Testing for Ethical AI*

1. **Create a Comprehensive Testing Protocol**:
   - Define testing objectives, including bias detection, fairness evaluation, and safety assurance.
   - Develop scenarios representing diverse use cases, including edge cases and outliers.
   - Document the results of all tests for accountability and improvement.

2. **Validate Fail-Safe Mechanisms for Emergency Scenarios**:
   - Test fail-safes and kill switches under simulated emergency conditions.
   - Ensure that fail-safes restore the system to a secure, non-harmful state.
   - Evaluate the reliability and accessibility of kill switches.

3. **Perform Third-Party Audits of Ethical Compliance**:
   - Engage independent experts to assess the system's

adherence to ethical principles.

– Validate testing results and identify potential blind spots.

– Incorporate third-party recommendations into system refinement.

• • • • • • • • • • • • • • • • • • • • • • • • • • • • • • • • • • • • • •

*Conclusion*

Rigorous testing is the cornerstone of ethical AI, ensuring systems are robust, fair, and safe for deployment. By identifying and mitigating biases, stress-testing for extreme scenarios, and designing effective fail-safes and monitoring mechanisms, organizations can build AI systems that uphold the highest ethical standards. This chapter provides a roadmap for thorough testing practices, safeguarding both users and the broader society.

• • • • • • • • • • • • • • • • • • • • • • • • • • • • • • • • • • • • •

# CHAPTER 8: EXPLAINABILITY IN AI SYSTEMS

## Introduction

Explainability in AI refers to the ability to make AI decision-making processes transparent and understandable to both technical and non-technical users. As AI systems increasingly influence critical decisions—ranging from healthcare diagnostics to credit approvals—their opacity can erode trust, hinder accountability, and amplify the risk of unintended consequences. This chapter explores the importance of explainability, techniques for enhancing interpretability, and strategies for balancing performance with transparency.

• • • • • • • • • • • • • • • • • • • • • • • • • • • • • • • • • • • • •

## Why Explainability Is Critical for Trust

Trust is a cornerstone of successful AI adoption, and explainability is a primary driver of trust. Without it, users, regulators, and other stakeholders may question the reliability, fairness, and safety of AI systems.

1. **Fostering User Confidence**:

   – When users understand how AI systems arrive at decisions, they are more likely to trust and accept those decisions.

   – Example: A user is more likely to trust a

loan application rejection if the AI explains the specific factors (e.g., income, credit score) influencing the decision.

2. **Facilitating Accountability**:

– Explainability ensures that developers and operators can identify and address errors or biases.

– Example: A self-driving car's decision to swerve can be scrutinized to determine whether it followed programmed ethical guidelines.

3. **Enabling Regulatory Compliance**:

– Many regulations, such as the General Data Protection Regulation (GDPR), require AI systems to provide explanations for automated decisions.

– Example: An AI system used for hiring must justify its selection process to comply with anti-discrimination laws.

4. **Reducing Ethical and Legal Risks**:

– Transparent systems reduce the likelihood of misuse or mistrust, safeguarding against lawsuits or reputational harm.

– Example: AI used in law enforcement must demonstrate fairness and avoid racial or socioeconomic biases.

• • • • • • • • • • • • • • • • • • • • • • • • • • • • • • •

*Techniques for Making AI Decisions Interpretable*
Achieving explainability involves a combination of technical methods, user-friendly tools, and clear communication strategies. Techniques vary based on the complexity of the AI model and the target audience.

1. **Simplified Models**:

– Use interpretable models, such as decision trees, linear

regression, or rule-based systems, when possible.

– **Pros**:

  • Easy to understand and explain.

  • Suitable for less complex tasks.

– **Cons**:

  • May sacrifice performance in tasks requiring complex representations.

2. **Post-Hoc Explainability Tools**:

– Tools that interpret complex models without altering their structure.

– **Examples**:

  • **SHAP (SHapley Additive exPlanations)**: Assigns importance values to features influencing a decision.

  • **LIME (Local Interpretable Model-Agnostic Explanations)**: Generates interpretable explanations for individual predictions.

– **Use Case**: Explaining predictions from a black-box neural network used for medical diagnostics.

3. **Visualization Techniques**:

– Represent AI processes and outputs visually to enhance user understanding.

– **Examples**:

  • Heatmaps for neural networks (e.g., highlighting areas of an image influencing a classification decision).

  • Graphical representations of decision paths in tree-based models.

4. **Interactive Dashboards**:

- Allow users to explore AI outputs dynamically.

- **Example**: A credit scoring system dashboard showing how changes in income or debt affect a user's score.

5. **Counterfactual Explanations**:

- Provide "what-if" scenarios to show how different inputs would lead to different outcomes.

- **Example**: For a rejected loan application, explaining how increasing income or reducing debt could change the decision.

6. **Natural Language Explanations**:

- Use AI to generate plain-language descriptions of decisions.

- **Example**: A chatbot explaining why it recommended a particular product based on user preferences.

• • • • • • • • • • • • • • • • • • • • • • • • • • • • • • •

*Balancing Performance with Explainability*

High-performance AI models, such as deep learning systems, often operate as black boxes, prioritizing accuracy over transparency. Balancing these trade-offs requires strategic decision-making.

1. **Choosing the Right Model**:

- For high-stakes applications (e.g., healthcare, law enforcement), prioritize explainable models even if they are slightly less accurate.

- For low-stakes applications (e.g., content recommendations), prioritize performance while using post-hoc explainability tools.

2. **Using Hybrid Approaches**:

- Combine interpretable models with black-box models to achieve both transparency and accuracy.

–     Example: A self-driving car might use interpretable decision trees for high-risk scenarios and deep learning for navigation.

3. **Segmenting Users**:

–     Provide varying levels of explanation based on user expertise.

–     Example: Technical users might receive detailed feature importance metrics, while non-technical users see simple visualizations or summaries.

4. **Continuous Feedback Loops**:

–     Monitor user satisfaction with explanations and refine explainability methods based on feedback.

–     Example: Regularly update the explanation features of an AI system based on user surveys.

• • • • • • • • • • • • • • • • • • • • • • • • • • • • • • • • • • •

*Checklist: Ensuring Explainability in AI Systems*

1. **Test User Comprehension of AI Outputs**:

–     Conduct usability studies to evaluate how well users understand AI decisions.

–     Use metrics like accuracy of user interpretations or time taken to understand explanations.

–     Adjust explanation methods based on feedback.

2. **Develop Documentation for Non-Technical Stakeholders**:

–     Provide clear, concise documentation explaining:

  •     The purpose and scope of the AI system.

  •     Key factors influencing decisions.

  •     Limitations and known biases.

–     Use accessible language and visual aids to ensure

comprehension.

3. **Integrate Explainability Tools**:

- Use tools like SHAP or LIME to interpret complex models.

- Implement user-friendly dashboards or visualizations to present outputs.

4. **Regularly Audit Explainability**:

- Evaluate the effectiveness of explainability methods periodically.

- Ensure compliance with legal and ethical requirements for transparency.

• • • • • • • • • • • • • • • • • • • • • • • • • • • • • • • • • •

*Conclusion*

Explainability is essential for building trust, ensuring accountability, and complying with ethical and legal standards in AI. By employing techniques to make decisions interpretable, balancing performance with transparency, and prioritizing user comprehension, organizations can bridge the gap between technical complexity and societal expectations. This chapter provides actionable guidance for integrating explainability into AI systems, fostering confidence and integrity in their deployment.

• • • • • • • • • • • • • • • • • • • • • • • • • • • • • • • • •

# CHAPTER 9: ETHICAL AI DEPLOYMENT

• • • • • • • • • • • • • • • • • • • • • • • • • • • • • • • • •

*Introduction*

Deploying AI systems into real-world environments brings significant responsibility. While design and development phases lay the foundation for ethical AI, deployment is where these principles are tested against complex, dynamic scenarios. Ethical AI deployment requires strict adherence to guidelines that prioritize human oversight, accountability, and continuous monitoring to address potential risks and ensure long-term compliance with ethical and societal standards.

This chapter provides a detailed framework for responsibly deploying AI systems, emphasizes the importance of human oversight in decision-critical systems, and outlines strategies for continuous monitoring post-deployment.

• • • • • • • • • • • • • • • • • • • • • • • • • • • • • • • • •

*Guidelines for Responsible AI Deployment*

The deployment phase is critical, as AI systems transition from controlled environments to real-world applications. The following guidelines ensure ethical and responsible deployment:

1.  **Conduct Pre-Deployment Testing**:

    –    Rigorously test the system in simulated real-world scenarios to identify potential risks.

    –    Validate ethical compliance through bias audits, fairness evaluations, and safety checks.

–      Example: Testing an AI-powered recruitment tool with diverse candidate profiles to ensure non-discrimination.

2. **Establish Deployment Protocols**:

–      Define a clear plan for rolling out the AI system, including pilot testing and gradual scaling.

–      Example: Deploying a healthcare diagnostic tool in a single hospital before expanding to an entire network.

3. **Transparency in Deployment**:

–      Communicate the AI system's purpose, capabilities, and limitations to all stakeholders, including end-users.

–      Provide detailed documentation outlining how decisions are made and potential risks.

–      Example: A self-driving car company publishing detailed safety protocols and decision-making processes.

4. **Stakeholder Engagement**:

–      Involve stakeholders (e.g., users, regulators, affected communities) in the deployment process.

–      Example: Engaging privacy advocates when deploying a surveillance AI system to ensure ethical data usage.

5. **Regulatory Compliance**:

–      Ensure the AI system adheres to applicable laws and regulations (e.g., GDPR, HIPAA).

–      Example: Ensuring an AI system handling health data complies with patient privacy laws.

• • • • • • • • • • • • • • • • • • • • • • • • • • • • • • • • •

*Ensuring Human Oversight in Decision-Critical Systems*
AI systems, especially those influencing critical decisions, must

operate under robust human oversight to prevent unintended harm.

1. **The Need for Oversight**:

   – AI systems lack the contextual understanding and ethical judgment of humans, making oversight essential for addressing unexpected scenarios.

2. **Key Strategies for Human Oversight**:

   – **Real-Time Supervision**:

   - Assign trained personnel to oversee AI operations and intervene when necessary.

   - Example: Monitoring autonomous drones to prevent unintended actions in sensitive areas.

   – **Decision-Aid Role**:

   - Use AI to augment, not replace, human decision-making.

   - Example: A medical diagnostic tool providing recommendations while leaving final decisions to physicians.

   – **Establish Escalation Protocols**:

   - Define clear procedures for escalating decisions to human operators.

   - Example: Flagging high-risk loan applications for manual review by banking staff.

3. **Oversight Tools and Mechanisms**:

   – **Audit Trails**:

   - Maintain detailed logs of AI decisions for accountability and review.

   – **Dashboard Interfaces**:

   - Provide user-friendly dashboards for real-time

monitoring of AI systems.

• • • • • • • • • • • • • • • • • • • • • • • • • • • • • • • • •

*Continuous Monitoring Post-Deployment*

AI systems do not operate in static environments. Continuous monitoring ensures that systems adapt to changing conditions and maintain compliance with ethical standards.

1. **The Importance of Continuous Monitoring:**

   - Detect and address biases, errors, or vulnerabilities that may emerge over time.

   - Ensure the system continues to meet ethical, legal, and performance standards.

2. **Key Components of Continuous Monitoring:**

   - **Performance Monitoring:**

     • Regularly assess system accuracy, efficiency, and reliability.

     • Example: Evaluating the predictive accuracy of a credit scoring model over time.

   - **Ethical Compliance Audits:**

     • Conduct periodic audits to ensure the system aligns with ethical guidelines.

     • Example: Reviewing the fairness of a hiring algorithm annually.

   - **Feedback Loops:**

     • Collect user feedback to identify and address issues proactively.

     • Example: Implementing a feedback mechanism for users to report concerns about an AI chatbot.

3. **Automation in Monitoring:**

   - Use AI tools to automate monitoring processes and

identify anomalies in real-time.

– Example: Anomaly detection algorithms flagging unusual activity in financial transactions.

4. **Updating and Improving AI Systems:**

– Continuously retrain and update models to adapt to new data and scenarios.

– Example: Updating a fraud detection system to address emerging tactics by malicious actors.

• • • • • • • • • • • • • • • • • • • • • • • • • • • • • • •

*Checklist: Ensuring Ethical AI Deployment*

1. **Develop an Oversight Plan for the Deployed System:**

– Define roles and responsibilities for human oversight at every stage.

– Establish real-time monitoring protocols and escalation procedures.

– Create tools and dashboards for supervisors to review AI decisions.

2. **Assign Responsibility for Ongoing Monitoring:**

– Designate a team or individual responsible for continuous monitoring.

– Provide training on ethical and operational oversight.

– Set regular review intervals for performance and ethical compliance.

3. **Test the System Before and After Deployment:**

– Conduct pre-deployment tests in controlled environments to validate safety and fairness.

– Perform post-deployment evaluations to identify issues arising in real-world use.

4. **Ensure Stakeholder Communication:**

–     Inform users and stakeholders about the system's purpose, limitations, and potential risks.

–     Establish channels for feedback and complaints.

• • • • • • • • • • • • • • • • • • • • • • • • • • • • • • • • •

*Conclusion*

Ethical AI deployment is a dynamic process that extends beyond the launch of a system. By adhering to guidelines, ensuring robust human oversight, and implementing continuous monitoring, organizations can minimize risks and maximize the positive impact of their AI systems. This chapter provides actionable strategies for deploying AI responsibly, ensuring alignment with ethical principles and societal expectations.

• • • • • • • • • • • • • • • • • • • • • • • • • • • • • • • • •

# CHAPTER 10: THE ROLE OF GLOBAL AI ETHICS AUTHORITIES

• • • • • • • • • • • • • • • • • • • • • • • • • • • • • • • • •

*Introduction*

The rapid development and deployment of artificial intelligence (AI) necessitate global coordination to address its ethical, legal, and societal implications. A global AI ethics authority can serve as a unified body to establish, enforce, and monitor international standards, ensuring responsible and equitable AI practices worldwide. This chapter provides a blueprint for creating such a body, explores methods for harmonizing international AI ethics standards, and offers strategies for overcoming cultural and legal differences among nations.

• • • • • • • • • • • • • • • • • • • • • • • • • • • • • • • • •

*Blueprint for Establishing a Global Regulatory Body*

A global regulatory body for AI ethics should act as a central authority for governance, policy-making, and compliance. Below are the foundational components for its establishment:

1. **Mission and Objectives**:

   – Promote ethical AI development and deployment globally.

   – Protect human rights and ensure AI benefits are distributed equitably.

   – Foster innovation while mitigating risks.

2. **Structural Design**:

– **Governing Council**:

- Composed of representatives from nations, industry leaders, ethicists, and civil society groups.

– **Technical Committees**:

- Focused on specific areas such as privacy, bias, transparency, and safety.

– **Advisory Board**:

- Includes academics, researchers, and non-governmental organizations for independent oversight.

3. **Core Functions**:

– **Standardization**:

- Develop and publish international AI ethics standards.

– **Regulation**:

- Certify AI systems that meet global ethical criteria.

– **Monitoring and Enforcement**:

- Conduct audits and impose penalties for non-compliance.

– **Capacity Building**:

- Provide resources and training for ethical AI practices worldwide.

4. **Funding and Resources**:

– Funded by contributions from member nations, multinational organizations, and industry stakeholders.

– Use resources for research, capacity building, and operational activities.

. . . . . . . . . . . . . . . . . . . . . . . . . . . . . . . . . . .

*Coordinating International AI Ethics Standards*

Global AI ethics standards are essential for ensuring consistency and trust in AI systems across borders. Establishing these standards requires collaboration among nations, industries, and other stakeholders.

1. **Developing Consensus-Based Standards**:

– Organize international summits to gather input from diverse stakeholders.

– Use consensus-driven approaches to balance competing interests and values.

2. **Key Areas for Standardization**:

– **Data Privacy**:

  • Define uniform data privacy standards aligned with principles such as consent and transparency.

  • Example: Aligning GDPR with privacy laws in other regions.

– **Bias and Fairness**:

  • Create metrics and benchmarks for measuring and mitigating bias.

  • Example: Establishing demographic parity as a universal fairness metric.

– **Safety and Security**:

  • Develop protocols for risk assessment, fail-safes, and emergency response mechanisms.

– **Transparency**:

  • Require AI systems to include explainability tools

and documentation.

3. **Enforcement Mechanisms**:

– Require certification from the global regulatory body for AI systems deployed internationally.

– Impose sanctions or restrictions on organizations failing to comply with standards.

• • • • • • • • • • • • • • • • • • • • • • • • • • • • • • • • •

*Overcoming Regional Cultural and Legal Differences*
Cultural and legal diversity among nations poses challenges to harmonizing AI ethics. Effective strategies are needed to bridge these gaps while respecting local values and norms.

1. **Understanding Regional Contexts**:

– Conduct cultural and legal analyses to identify regional priorities and constraints.

– Example: Balancing freedom of expression with content moderation in countries with differing laws.

2. **Promoting Mutual Respect and Collaboration**:

– Encourage cross-cultural dialogue to foster understanding and cooperation.

– Example: Collaborating on AI projects that address global challenges, such as climate change or healthcare.

3. **Flexible Standards with Core Principles**:

– Develop adaptable frameworks that allow for regional customization while maintaining core ethical principles.

– Example: A global data privacy framework that permits variations in implementation while ensuring fundamental protections.

4. **Capacity Building in Developing Regions**:

–    Provide technical and financial support to ensure that all nations can participate in and benefit from ethical AI.

–    Example: Offering training programs on AI ethics for policymakers in low-income countries.

• • • • • • • • • • • • • • • • • • • • • • • • • • • • • • • • • • • • •

*Checklist: Ensuring Compliance with Global AI Ethics Standards*

1.  **Register Systems with Global or Regional Oversight Bodies**:

–    Ensure all AI systems are registered with the appropriate oversight body before deployment.

–    Provide documentation of compliance with ethical guidelines.

2.  **Align Development Practices with International Standards**:

–    Incorporate global ethical standards into the AI development lifecycle.

–    Regularly review updates to international guidelines and adjust practices accordingly.

3.  **Establish Internal Compliance Teams**:

–    Create dedicated teams within organizations to monitor adherence to global standards.

–    Conduct internal audits and maintain records for transparency.

4.  **Engage with Global Regulatory Bodies**:

–    Participate in discussions, workshops, and summits organized by the global AI ethics authority.

–    Provide feedback and collaborate on the development of new standards.

• • • • • • • • • • • • • • • • • • • • • • • • • • • • • • • • • •

*Conclusion*

The establishment of a global AI ethics authority is crucial for fostering international collaboration and ensuring the responsible development and deployment of AI. By creating a unified regulatory body, coordinating international standards, and addressing regional differences, the global community can harness the transformative potential of AI while safeguarding human rights and societal values. This chapter outlines the roadmap for achieving this vision, emphasizing the importance of cooperation, transparency, and accountability in shaping the future of ethical AI.

• • • • • • • • • • • • • • • • • • • • • • • • • • • • • • • • • •

# CHAPTER 11: ENFORCING ETHICAL AI

● ● ● ● ● ● ● ● ● ● ● ● ● ● ● ● ● ● ● ● ● ● ● ● ● ● ●

## Introduction

Enforcing ethical AI practices is as critical as designing and deploying ethical systems. Without robust enforcement mechanisms, even the most carefully crafted guidelines and standards risk being ignored or circumvented. Enforcement ensures accountability, deters unethical behavior, and protects society from potential harm caused by AI systems. This chapter explores penalties for unethical practices, the importance of real-time intervention systems, and mechanisms to safeguard whistleblowers who expose violations. By embedding enforcement into the AI lifecycle, organizations can ensure sustained compliance with ethical principles.

● ● ● ● ● ● ● ● ● ● ● ● ● ● ● ● ● ● ● ● ● ● ● ● ● ● ●

## Penalties for Unethical AI Practices

Penalties serve as deterrents and accountability measures for organizations and individuals violating ethical AI standards. Effective penalty systems must be proportional, transparent, and enforceable.

1. **Types of Penalties**:

   – **Financial Penalties**:

     • Fines proportional to the severity of the violation

and its impact.

- Example: Significant fines for companies using biased hiring algorithms leading to discrimination.

- **Operational Restrictions**:

    - Temporary or permanent bans on deploying AI systems found to be unethical.

    - Example: Suspending a surveillance AI system misused for unauthorized mass data collection.

- **Criminal Liability**:

    - Legal action against individuals or entities responsible for malicious or grossly negligent AI practices.

    - Example: Prosecution of developers knowingly deploying deepfake tools for fraud.

- **Reputational Damage**:

    - Public disclosure of violations to hold organizations accountable in the eyes of stakeholders.

    - Example: Publishing non-compliance reports for transparency.

2. **Enforcement Mechanisms**:

- **Regulatory Oversight**:

    - National or global AI ethics authorities to monitor compliance and impose penalties.

- **Third-Party Audits**:

    - Independent reviews to assess ethical adherence and recommend penalties for violations.

3. **Case Study**:

- **Example**: A facial recognition system deployed by a tech company was found to have significant racial biases, leading to wrongful detentions. Regulatory authorities fined the company $10 million and required immediate withdrawal of the system.

. . . . . . . . . . . . . . . . . . . . . . . . . . . . . . . . . . . . . .

*Real-Time Intervention Systems (e.g., Kill Switches)*

Real-time intervention systems are critical for preventing or mitigating harm when AI systems behave unpredictably or violate ethical guidelines.

1. **Purpose of Real-Time Intervention:**

   - Provide immediate control over AI systems to prevent harm or ethical breaches.

   - Ensure systems can be shut down or corrected during emergencies.

2. **Key Components of Intervention Systems:**

   - **Kill Switches:**

     - Mechanisms for instant shutdown of the AI system.

     - Example: Disabling an autonomous weapon system if it targets civilians.

   - **Pause Functions:**

     - Temporarily halt operations to review and rectify issues.

     - Example: Pausing a financial AI system to investigate suspicious transactions.

   - **Fail-Safe Mechanisms:**

     - Automatic reversion to a safe state during malfunctions.

     - Example: An autonomous vehicle returning to a

safe stop position upon detecting sensor failures.

3. **Design and Implementation**:

–       Build intervention mechanisms into the system architecture during the design phase.

–       Assign control access to authorized personnel to prevent misuse.

–       Test intervention systems regularly to ensure functionality.

4. **Case Study**:

–       **Example**: A drone delivery system with a kill switch successfully prevented a collision when it malfunctioned and veered off its programmed route.

• • • • • • • • • • • • • • • • • • • • • • • • • • • • • • • • • •

*Mechanisms for Whistleblower Protection*

Whistleblowers play a vital role in exposing unethical AI practices, but they often face significant risks, including retaliation and legal repercussions. Establishing safe reporting channels and robust protection measures encourages accountability and transparency.

1. **Importance of Whistleblower Protections**:

–       Prevents suppression of critical information about unethical practices.

–       Promotes a culture of transparency and ethical responsibility.

2. **Key Elements of Whistleblower Mechanisms**:

–       **Anonymous Reporting Channels**:

•       Platforms enabling individuals to report violations without fear of identification.

•       Example: Encrypted reporting tools that ensure anonymity.

– **Legal Protections**:

- Laws shielding whistleblowers from retaliation, such as job termination or legal action.

- Example: Anti-retaliation clauses in national labor laws.

– **Support Systems**:

- Counseling and legal aid for whistleblowers facing challenges.

- Example: Providing legal representation for employees reporting unsafe AI practices.

3. **Building Trust in Whistleblower Systems**:

– Communicate the availability and security of reporting channels.

– Ensure prompt and fair investigation of reported violations.

– Celebrate successful whistleblowing cases to encourage others.

4. **Case Study**:

– **Example**: A whistleblower revealed that an AI-powered content moderation tool was suppressing legitimate political discourse. Following the report, the company revised the algorithm and implemented better oversight.

• • • • • • • • • • • • • • • • • • • • • • • • • • • • • • • •

*Checklist: Enforcing Ethical AI*

1. **Incorporate Real-Time Intervention Systems in All Deployments**:

– Design and implement kill switches, pause functions, and fail-safes in all AI systems.

–     Assign control access to trained and authorized personnel.

–     Test intervention mechanisms periodically to ensure they function as intended.

2. **Create Safe Channels for Reporting Ethical Violations**:

–     Develop secure and anonymous reporting platforms.

–     Communicate the existence of whistleblower protections to employees and stakeholders.

–     Establish policies to investigate reports promptly and fairly.

3. **Enforce Penalties for Unethical Practices**:

–     Collaborate with regulatory authorities to impose fines, restrictions, or legal actions.

–     Publicize enforcement actions to deter future violations.

4. **Conduct Regular Audits**:

–     Partner with independent third parties for periodic ethical reviews.

–     Address identified issues promptly to maintain compliance.

• • • • • • • • • • • • • • • • • • • • • • • • • • • • • • •

*Conclusion*

Enforcement is the linchpin of ethical AI governance, ensuring that systems remain accountable and aligned with societal values. Through effective penalties, robust real-time intervention systems, and strong whistleblower protections, organizations can deter unethical practices and safeguard against harm. This chapter provides actionable strategies for embedding enforcement into the AI lifecycle, fostering a culture of accountability and trust.

# CHAPTER 12: AUTONOMY IN AI SYSTEMS

• • • • • • • • • • • • • • • • • • • • • • • • • • • • • • • • • • • •

*Introduction*

Autonomous AI systems—those capable of operating with minimal human intervention—have become pivotal in fields ranging from transportation to healthcare. While autonomy enables efficiency and scalability, it introduces significant ethical, operational, and safety challenges. Defining clear boundaries for AI autonomy is critical to prevent harm, ensure accountability, and maintain human oversight.

This chapter explores the ethical implications of autonomous AI systems, examines challenges in key domains such as vehicles, robotics, and drones, and analyzes case studies of failures to derive actionable lessons. Practical strategies and a checklist for safe deployment are also provided.

• • • • • • • • • • • • • • • • • • • • • • • • • • • • • • • • • • • •

*Defining Limits for AI Autonomy*

The degree of autonomy granted to an AI system must align with the system's use case, societal impact, and potential risks. Setting limits involves balancing the benefits of autonomy with the need for human oversight.

1. **Levels of Autonomy**:

    – **Manual Control**: Human operators handle all decisions, with AI providing support (e.g., diagnostic tools).

- **Assisted Autonomy**: AI performs specific tasks under human supervision (e.g., autopilot in aircraft).

- **Full Autonomy**: AI operates independently, making all decisions without human intervention (e.g., fully autonomous vehicles).

2. **Key Factors in Setting Limits**:

- **Context of Use**:

  - High-stakes applications (e.g., surgery, warfare) require stricter oversight than low-stakes applications (e.g., content recommendations).

- **Risk Assessment**:

  - Evaluate the potential for harm, misuse, or unintended consequences.

- **Accountability**:

  - Clearly define responsibility for the system's actions at each level of autonomy.

3. **Dynamic Autonomy**:

- Implement systems capable of adjusting autonomy levels based on situational complexity.

- Example: A delivery drone operating autonomously in open spaces but requiring human oversight in crowded areas.

• • • • • • • • • • • • • • • • • • • • • • • • • • • • • • • •

*Ethical Challenges in Autonomous Systems*

Autonomous systems pose unique ethical challenges across various domains. Below are key issues and examples from specific applications.

1. **Autonomous Vehicles**:

- **Ethical Challenge**: Decision-making in life-and-death scenarios.

- Example: A self-driving car must choose between colliding with a pedestrian or endangering its passengers.

– **Solution**:

- Program vehicles with ethical frameworks (e.g., prioritizing safety of the greatest number).
- Ensure decisions are transparent and explainable.

2. **Robotics in Healthcare**:

– **Ethical Challenge**: Balancing efficiency with empathy.

- Example: Robots assisting elderly patients may lack the human touch necessary for emotional support.

– **Solution**:

- Design systems that integrate human intervention for tasks requiring empathy or judgment.
- Use ethical guidelines to ensure respect for patient dignity.

3. **Autonomous Drones**:

– **Ethical Challenge**: Privacy and security concerns.

- Example: Drones used for surveillance may infringe on individual privacy rights.

– **Solution**:

- Limit drone usage in sensitive areas and ensure compliance with privacy laws.
- Implement robust encryption to protect data.

• • • • • • • • • • • • • • • • • • • • • • • • • • • • • • • • • • • •

*Case Studies of Autonomous System Failures*

Examining past failures of autonomous systems provides

critical insights into potential pitfalls and necessary safeguards.

1. **Case Study 1: Uber's Autonomous Vehicle Accident (2018)**:

   – **Incident**: An autonomous vehicle struck and killed a pedestrian during testing.

   – **Issues Identified**:

     • Inadequate object recognition systems.

     • Lack of timely human intervention.

   – **Lessons Learned**:

     • Ensure robust testing for edge cases and fail-safes.

     • Maintain active human oversight during testing phases.

2. **Case Study 2: Boeing 737 MAX Crashes (2018-2019)**:

   – **Incident**: Faulty automation in the MCAS (Maneuvering Characteristics Augmentation System) led to two catastrophic crashes.

   – **Issues Identified**:

     • Over-reliance on automation without adequate pilot training.

     • Poor system design and testing.

   – **Lessons Learned**:

     • Balance automation with user training and control.

     • Implement thorough system testing and independent audits.

3. **Case Study 3: Robot Surgery Malfunctions**:

   – **Incident**: Surgical robots caused complications due to mechanical failures and inadequate surgeon training.

- **Issues Identified:**
  - Lack of fail-safes for critical procedures.
  - Insufficient understanding of robotic limitations by operators.
- **Lessons Learned:**
  - Include robust fail-safes and extensive training programs for operators.
  - Regularly update and maintain systems to prevent malfunctions.

• • • • • • • • • • • • • • • • • • • • • • • • • • • • • • •

*Practical Strategies for Safe Autonomy*

To address the challenges and risks of autonomous systems, organizations should adopt the following strategies:

1. **Define Clear Use Cases:**
   - Specify tasks the system is authorized to perform autonomously.
   - Example: A delivery robot's autonomy is limited to navigating sidewalks but requires human approval for package delivery.

2. **Continuous Risk Assessment:**
   - Regularly evaluate risks associated with system autonomy.
   - Use simulation tools to anticipate potential failures in diverse scenarios.

3. **Human-in-the-Loop Models:**
   - Maintain human oversight for critical decisions or high-risk tasks.
   - Example: A drone delivering medical supplies alerts a human operator for route changes in high-traffic areas.

4. **Regular Updates and Maintenance**:

- Continuously update systems to address vulnerabilities or improve performance.

- Example: Updating an autonomous vehicle's software to adapt to new traffic regulations.

5. **Transparency and Accountability**:

- Ensure decisions made by autonomous systems are explainable and auditable.

- Assign accountability for failures or misuse.

• • • • • • • • • • • • • • • • • • • • • • • • • • • • • • • • • • • • • •

*Checklist: Ensuring Ethical Autonomy in AI Systems*

1. **Document Autonomy Boundaries for Each Use Case**:

- Define the scope and limitations of autonomy for the system.

- Specify roles and responsibilities for human operators and AI components.

2. **Test Systems Under Scenarios Requiring Human Intervention**:

- Simulate edge cases where human input is necessary.

- Evaluate system performance during transitions between autonomous and manual control.

3. **Implement Fail-Safes for Autonomous Operations**:

- Design mechanisms for immediate system shutdown or manual override.

- Regularly test fail-safe mechanisms to ensure reliability.

4. **Provide User Training and Education**:

- Train users on the system's capabilities, limitations, and intervention procedures.

–        Example: Training pilots on how to override autonomous flight systems.

5.  **Conduct Periodic Audits**:

–        Partner with independent auditors to evaluate autonomy limits and compliance with ethical standards.

–        Document and address audit findings promptly.

• • • • • • • • • • • • • • • • • • • • • • • • • • • • • • • •

*Conclusion*

Autonomous AI systems have the potential to transform industries and improve lives, but their deployment comes with significant ethical and safety challenges. By defining clear limits for autonomy, addressing domain-specific ethical concerns, and learning from past failures, organizations can mitigate risks and ensure responsible use. This chapter provides a roadmap for achieving safe and ethical autonomy in AI systems, emphasizing the importance of transparency, accountability, and human oversight.

• • • • • • • • • • • • • • • • • • • • • • • • • • • • • • • •

# CHAPTER 13:
# GENERATIVE AI
# AND DEEPFAKES

- - - - - - - - - - - - - - - - - - - - - - - - -

*Introduction*

Generative AI, capable of creating realistic images, videos, text, and audio, has revolutionized creative industries, education, and research. However, this transformative technology also brings significant risks, such as the propagation of misinformation, fraud, and privacy violations. Among its most concerning applications are deepfakes—AI-generated content that manipulates media to mimic real individuals or events, often for malicious purposes. This chapter examines the risks associated with generative AI, explores strategies for identifying and mitigating harmful outputs, and provides ethical guidelines for developers to ensure responsible innovation.

- - - - - - - - - - - - - - - - - - - - - - - - -

*Risks of Misinformation and Misuse*

Generative AI's power to create lifelike content has opened doors to both positive applications and malicious exploitation. Below are some of the most pressing risks:

1. **Misinformation and Disinformation**:

   – **Definition**:

       • Misinformation: Unintentional spread of false or misleading information.

- Disinformation: Intentional creation and dissemination of false information to deceive.

  – **Impact**:

- Erodes trust in institutions, individuals, and the media.

- Influences public opinion and democratic processes.

  – **Example**:

- Deepfake videos showing political leaders making false statements to sway elections.

2. **Fraud and Cybercrime**:

  – **Risks**:

- Generative AI can produce voice deepfakes for phishing attacks, impersonating trusted individuals.

- AI-generated text can create convincing fake emails or contracts.

  – **Example**:

- A deepfake voice used to scam a company into transferring funds to a fraudulent account.

3. **Privacy Violations**:

  – **Risks**:

- Deepfake images or videos can exploit individuals' likenesses without consent.

- AI-generated "revenge porn" or false allegations can damage reputations.

  – **Example**:

- Celebrities targeted with AI-generated explicit content.

4. **Loss of Authenticity**:

– **Risks**:

- Overreliance on AI-generated content diminishes the value of genuine creativity.

- Saturation of deepfake content undermines the reliability of legitimate media.

– **Example**:

- A surge in fake news videos making it difficult to discern real from fake.

• • • • • • • • • • • • • • • • • • • • • • • • • • • • • • • • •

*Identifying and Combatting Harmful AI-Generated Content*
To mitigate the risks associated with generative AI, robust methods for detection, monitoring, and intervention are essential.

1. **Detection Techniques**:

– **Watermarking**:

- Embed digital watermarks in generative outputs to verify authenticity.

- Example: A watermark in AI-generated images indicating their origin.

– **AI Detection Tools**:

- Develop and deploy AI models trained to identify deepfakes and generative outputs.

- Example: Facebook's deepfake detection tool trained on large datasets.

– **Metadata Analysis**:

- Attach metadata to AI-generated content for traceability.

- Example: Storing creation timestamps and source

model identifiers.

2. **Public Awareness Campaigns**:

–     Educate the public about the existence and risks of generative AI and deepfakes.

–     Provide tools and resources for individuals to verify content authenticity.

–     Example: Fact-checking websites and browser extensions for fake news detection.

3. **Monitoring and Reporting**:

–   **Continuous Monitoring**:

  •     Track the spread of AI-generated content on social media and other platforms.

  •     Use AI tools to flag suspicious content in real-time.

–   **Reporting Mechanisms**:

  •     Create accessible channels for reporting harmful or unethical generative content.

  •     Collaborate with platforms to take down identified deepfakes.

4. **Legal and Regulatory Measures**:

–     Enforce stricter laws against the misuse of generative AI.

–     Example: Introducing penalties for creating deepfakes without consent.

• • • • • • • • • • • • • • • • • • • • • • • • • • • • • • • • • • • •

*Ethical Guidelines for Generative AI Developers*
Developers of generative AI systems hold a crucial responsibility to mitigate risks and promote ethical practices.

1. **Design Principles**:

–     Build systems with safeguards to prevent misuse.

–    Example: Implementing usage restrictions for AI models trained on sensitive data.

2. **Transparency**:

–    Clearly label AI-generated content to distinguish it from real media.

–    Provide users with the option to disclose the generative nature of content.

3. **Access Control**:

–    Restrict access to generative AI tools to prevent misuse.

–    Example: API usage limited to verified accounts with clear terms of use.

4. **Bias Mitigation**:

–    Ensure training datasets are diverse and inclusive to prevent biased outputs.

–    Regularly audit models for unintended biases.

5. **Collaboration and Accountability**:

–    Work with regulators, platforms, and other developers to create unified standards.

–    Example: Participating in industry coalitions like the Partnership on AI.

• • • • • • • • • • • • • • • • • • • • • • • • • • • • • • • •

*Checklist: Ensuring Responsible Use of Generative AI*

1. **Implement Watermarking for Generative Outputs**:

–    Embed visible or invisible markers to identify content as AI-generated.

–    Regularly update watermarking techniques to stay ahead of forgery methods.

2. **Monitor Public Usage for Ethical Compliance**:

- Use AI tools to monitor platforms for harmful or unethical uses of generative outputs.

- Set up alert systems for flagged content and collaborate with platforms for timely removal.

3. **Educate Users on Ethical Use**:

- Provide guidelines and examples of acceptable use cases for generative AI tools.

- Offer training sessions or resources for responsible content creation.

4. **Collaborate with Regulators**:

- Engage with policymakers to develop laws addressing generative AI misuse.

- Ensure compliance with legal standards for content authenticity and privacy.

5. **Regularly Update Detection Tools**:

- Continuously improve tools and algorithms for identifying deepfakes and harmful generative outputs.

- Share advancements with the wider AI community to strengthen defenses.

• • • • • • • • • • • • • • • • • • • • • • • • • • • • • • • •

*Conclusion*

Generative AI has vast potential to innovate and enhance creativity, but it also poses significant risks if misused. Developers and stakeholders must adopt proactive strategies to identify and mitigate harmful content while adhering to robust ethical guidelines. By implementing measures such as watermarking, continuous monitoring, and public education, the risks of generative AI can be effectively managed, ensuring its positive contributions outweigh the potential for harm.

• • • • • • • • • • • • • • • • • • • • • • • • • • • • • • • •

# CHAPTER 14:
# EMOTION AI AND
# MANIPULATION

• • • • • • • • • • • • • • • • • • • • • • • • • • • • • • • •

*Introduction*

Emotion AI, also known as affective computing, refers to systems capable of recognizing, interpreting, and simulating human emotions. By analyzing facial expressions, voice tones, text patterns, and physiological signals, Emotion AI can provide personalized user experiences in applications like customer service, mental health support, and education. However, its ability to manipulate emotions also raises significant ethical concerns. This chapter explores the ethical considerations of emotional simulation, guidelines to prevent manipulation and exploitation, and actionable strategies to ensure ethical use of Emotion AI.

• • • • • • • • • • • • • • • • • • • • • • • • • • • • • • • •

*Ethical Considerations in Emotional Simulation*

Emotion AI's ability to simulate and respond to human emotions presents unique ethical challenges. While it has transformative potential, it must be deployed responsibly to avoid unintended consequences.

1. **Understanding Emotional Boundaries**:

   –   **What it can do**:

   •   Recognize user emotions to tailor responses.

- Simulate empathy for customer service or mental health applications.

– **Ethical Risks:**

- Crossing boundaries by exploiting vulnerabilities, such as influencing purchasing decisions through emotional appeals.

2. **Consent and Transparency:**

– Users must be aware when interacting with Emotion AI and provide informed consent.

– Example: Informing users if a chatbot uses sentiment analysis to influence dialogue.

3. **Bias in Emotional Recognition:**

– Emotion AI systems may misinterpret emotions due to biases in training data.

– Example: Cultural differences in emotional expression can lead to inaccuracies.

4. **Emotional Manipulation:**

– Emotion AI could be exploited to manipulate users for profit or influence.

– Example: Using sentiment analysis to pressure users into making impulsive purchases.

5. **Psychological Impacts:**

– Prolonged interactions with Emotion AI may affect user well-being, creating dependency or blurring the line between human and AI interaction.

• • • • • • • • • • • • • • • • • • • • • • • • • • • • • • • • • • •

*Guidelines for Avoiding Manipulation and Exploitation*

To mitigate risks, developers and organizations must adhere to strict ethical guidelines when designing and deploying Emotion

AI systems.

1. **Transparency in Emotional AI Interactions**:

    – Clearly label interactions with Emotion AI to ensure users are aware.

    – Example: A customer service chatbot explicitly stating it uses emotion recognition to improve responses.

2. **Obtain Informed Consent**:

    – Inform users about the system's capabilities, data collection practices, and intended use of emotional data.

    – Provide users with the option to opt-out of emotional data analysis.

3. **Limit Emotional Influence**:

    – Avoid leveraging emotional insights for exploitative purposes, such as manipulating spending behavior or influencing political opinions.

    – Example: Prohibiting the use of Emotion AI in advertising campaigns targeting vulnerable populations.

4. **Cultural Sensitivity**:

    – Train systems on diverse datasets to minimize cultural biases in emotion recognition.

    – Regularly audit systems to ensure fairness across demographic groups.

5. **Respect User Privacy**:

    – Anonymize emotional data to protect user identities.

    – Example: Aggregating emotional trends without linking them to individual users.

6. **Monitor Psychological Impact**:

- Study the long-term effects of Emotion AI on users to identify and mitigate potential harm.

- Example: Researching whether prolonged chatbot use affects social interactions.

7. **Establish Ethical Boundaries**:

- Define acceptable and unacceptable use cases for Emotion AI.

- Prohibit use in areas prone to exploitation, such as gambling or predatory lending.

• • • • • • • • • • • • • • • • • • • • • • • • • • • • • • • • • • • •

*Applications and Use Cases of Emotion AI*

1. **Mental Health Support**:

- Emotion AI can identify signs of stress, anxiety, or depression and provide early interventions.

- Example: AI chatbots offering emotional support during crises.

2. **Education**:

- Personalized learning systems adapting to students' emotional states for better engagement.

- Example: Adjusting difficulty levels when detecting frustration.

3. **Customer Service**:

- Enhancing user experience by recognizing dissatisfaction or frustration.

- Example: A call center AI transferring calls to a human agent when detecting user distress.

4. **Marketing and Advertising**:

- Tailoring advertisements based on emotional responses to maximize impact.

– Ethical Concern: Avoid using insights to exploit vulnerabilities.

• • • • • • • • • • • • • • • • • • • • • • • • • • • • • • • •

## Case Studies of Ethical and Unethical Use

1. **Ethical Use: AI for Mental Health**:

– A mental health platform uses Emotion AI to detect signs of depression and recommend professional help.

– Key Practices: Informed consent, anonymized data, and clear boundaries for intervention.

2. **Unethical Use: Manipulative Advertising**:

– A retail website uses Emotion AI to identify users' emotional states and pressure them into purchasing during moments of vulnerability.

– Ethical Failures: Lack of transparency, exploitative practices, and no opt-out mechanism.

• • • • • • • • • • • • • • • • • • • • • • • • • • • • • • • •

## Checklist: Ensuring Ethical Use of Emotion AI

1. **Label Emotional AI Interactions Transparently**:

– Inform users when Emotion AI is involved in interactions.

– Example: Clearly stating, "This chatbot uses emotion recognition to enhance responses."

2. **Conduct Regular Reviews of User Experience**:

– Periodically assess how users interact with the system to identify and address potential exploitation or manipulation.

– Example: Monitoring feedback on whether users feel pressured or manipulated.

3. **Implement Privacy Safeguards**:

–    Use data anonymization and encryption to protect emotional data.

–    Limit access to sensitive data within the organization.

4. **Develop Ethical Use Policies**:

–    Establish internal guidelines outlining acceptable applications of Emotion AI.

–    Example: Prohibiting its use in gambling or other high-risk industries.

5. **Audit for Cultural Biases**:

–    Regularly test systems for biases in emotional recognition across diverse demographics.

–    Example: Ensuring the system does not misinterpret emotions due to cultural differences.

6. **Monitor Psychological Impact**:

–    Conduct studies to assess the long-term effects of Emotion AI on user well-being.

–    Example: Tracking whether users become overly reliant on Emotion AI tools.

• • • • • • • • • • • • • • • • • • • • • • • • • • • • • • • • • •

*Conclusion*

Emotion AI represents a powerful tool for enhancing user experiences and addressing emotional needs in areas like mental health, education, and customer service. However, its potential for manipulation and exploitation requires strict ethical safeguards. By adhering to guidelines for transparency, informed consent, and cultural sensitivity, and by regularly reviewing user experiences, developers and organizations can ensure Emotion AI is deployed responsibly and ethically.

• • • • • • • • • • • • • • • • • • • • • • • • • • • • • • • • • •

# CHAPTER 15: WEAPONIZATION OF AI

- - - - - - - - - - - - - - - - - - - - - - - - - - - - - - - -

*Introduction*

Artificial intelligence is reshaping modern warfare, enabling advanced defense systems, autonomous weapons, and enhanced military strategies. While these developments promise to revolutionize security and defense, they also raise critical ethical and legal concerns. The weaponization of AI introduces unprecedented risks, including potential misuse, escalation of conflicts, and challenges to international laws governing warfare. This chapter explores the role of international treaties, ethical guidelines for defense-related AI, and strategies to ensure responsible development and deployment of military AI systems.

- - - - - - - - - - - - - - - - - - - - - - - - - - - - - - - -

*International Treaties and Ethical Constraints for AI in Warfare*

Existing international frameworks provide guidance on the ethical use of AI in military applications. However, their scope must evolve to address the unique challenges posed by autonomous and intelligent systems.

1. **Key International Treaties and Frameworks**:

   – **Geneva Conventions**:

      • Establish rules for humane treatment in armed

conflicts.

- Relevance: Prohibit AI systems that target civilians or cause unnecessary suffering.

– **Convention on Certain Conventional Weapons (CCW)**:

- Regulates the use of specific weapons deemed excessively injurious or indiscriminate.

- Relevance: Addresses autonomous weapons through ongoing debates on their legality and regulation.

– **United Nations Charter**:

- Prohibits aggression and emphasizes peaceful resolution of conflicts.

- Relevance: Limits the deployment of AI systems that could provoke unnecessary escalation.

2. **Ethical Principles for AI in Warfare**:

– **Distinction**:

- AI systems must differentiate between combatants and civilians.

- Example: Autonomous drones must identify legitimate military targets accurately.

– **Proportionality**:

- AI use should minimize harm and not cause excessive damage relative to military objectives.

– **Accountability**:

- Human operators must retain control and responsibility for AI decisions in warfare.

3. **Challenges to Existing Treaties**:

– Lack of consensus on the definition and regulation of autonomous weapons.

- Difficulty in attributing responsibility for AI-induced actions in conflicts.

- Rapid technological advancements outpacing legislative updates.

• • • • • • • • • • • • • • • • • • • • • • • • • • • • • • • • •

*Guidelines for Developing Defense-Related AI Responsibly*
To address the ethical and legal complexities of military AI, developers and governments must follow strict guidelines during research, development, and deployment.

1. **Human Oversight and Decision-Making**:

   - AI systems should augment, not replace, human decision-making in warfare.

   - Example: Retaining human authorization for deploying lethal autonomous weapons.

2. **Accountability Mechanisms**:

   - Assign clear responsibility for AI actions, ensuring accountability at all levels.

   - Example: Creating audit trails for decisions made by AI in combat scenarios.

3. **Bias and Fairness in Military AI**:

   - Train AI systems on diverse datasets to avoid biases that could lead to unjust actions.

   - Example: Ensuring an AI targeting system does not disproportionately impact certain regions or groups.

4. **Transparency in Development and Use**:

   - Maintain transparency with allies, regulators, and international bodies about the capabilities and limitations of military AI systems.

   - Example: Sharing technical details about autonomous drones with oversight bodies.

5. **Limiting Escalation Risks**:

–    Design AI systems with fail-safes to prevent unintended escalation of conflicts.

–    Example: Ensuring autonomous systems cannot independently initiate attacks without human intervention.

• • • • • • • • • • • • • • • • • • • • • • • • • • • • • • • • • •

*Case Studies of Weaponized AI*

Examining past and hypothetical scenarios highlights the importance of ethical safeguards in military AI.

1. **Case Study 1: Autonomous Drones in Combat**:

–    **Scenario**: In 2020, reports surfaced of autonomous drones allegedly used in Libya, targeting combatants without human oversight.

–    **Key Issues**:

•    Lack of human control in target identification and engagement.

•    Potential violation of international humanitarian law.

–    **Lessons Learned**:

•    Implement robust oversight and control mechanisms.

•    Ensure compliance with international treaties.

2. **Case Study 2: Cyber Warfare and AI**:

–    **Scenario**: AI-driven cyberattacks target critical infrastructure, disrupting civilian life.

–    **Key Issues**:

•    Difficulty attributing attacks to specific actors.

•    Escalation risks due to retaliatory actions.

- **Lessons Learned**:

  - Strengthen international collaboration on cybersecurity norms.

  - Develop defensive AI systems to mitigate such risks.

3. **Case Study 3: Predictive AI in Defense**:

- **Scenario**: An AI system predicts enemy movements, leading to preemptive strikes.

- **Key Issues**:

  - Reliance on potentially flawed predictions.

  - Ethical concerns over preemptive actions.

- **Lessons Learned**:

  - Balance predictive capabilities with human judgment.

  - Ensure transparency in how predictions are generated and acted upon.

• • • • • • • • • • • • • • • • • • • • • • • • • • • • • • • • •

*Checklist: Ensuring Ethical Weaponization of AI*

1. **Validate Defense-Related AI Systems with International Treaties**:

- Review system designs for compliance with Geneva Conventions, CCW, and other relevant frameworks.

- Engage legal experts to assess potential violations of humanitarian law.

2. **Develop Internal Ethical Safeguards for Military Applications**:

- Establish ethics review boards within defense organizations.

- Regularly audit AI systems for bias, accountability, and

proportionality.

3. **Maintain Human Oversight:**

–   Ensure human operators retain ultimate authority over critical decisions, particularly in lethal applications.

–   Train military personnel to understand AI systems and their limitations.

4. **Implement Robust Fail-Safes:**

–   Design fail-safe mechanisms to deactivate or override AI systems in emergencies.

–   Test fail-safes under realistic scenarios to ensure reliability.

5. **Foster International Collaboration:**

–   Participate in global discussions on AI ethics in warfare.

–   Share best practices and collaborate on developing norms and standards.

6. **Monitor Post-Deployment Impact:**

–   Continuously assess the impact of deployed systems on combatants, civilians, and infrastructure.

–   Use feedback to refine ethical guidelines and system designs.

• • • • • • • • • • • • • • • • • • • • • • • • • • • • • • • • • •

*Conclusion*

The weaponization of AI presents profound ethical and legal challenges that require immediate and sustained attention. By adhering to international treaties, implementing robust safeguards, and fostering global collaboration, governments and developers can ensure that AI enhances security without compromising humanity's values. This chapter provides actionable guidelines for responsibly navigating the complexities of military AI, emphasizing the importance of accountability, transparency, and restraint.

• • • • • • • • • • • • • • • • • • • • • • • • • • • • • • • • • • • • • • •

# CHAPTER 16: RECURSIVE MONITORING AND SELF-REGULATION

*Introduction*

Recursive monitoring and self-regulation represent a paradigm shift in AI development, where systems are designed to continuously evaluate their performance and compliance with ethical principles. These capabilities enable AI to adapt to new challenges and evolving standards without constant human intervention, ensuring sustained accountability and reliability. This chapter explores the design principles, benefits, and challenges of self-regulating AI systems and provides actionable strategies for their development and maintenance.

*Designing AI Systems That Self-Monitor for Ethical Compliance*

Self-monitoring systems are AI solutions equipped with mechanisms to evaluate their own decisions, detect potential issues, and take corrective actions. Integrating these capabilities requires a multi-layered approach.

1. **Key Features of Self-Monitoring Systems**:

   – **Ethical Compliance Auditing**:

      • Regularly check decisions and actions against

predefined ethical guidelines.

- Example: An AI system evaluating whether its hiring recommendations comply with anti-discrimination laws.

- **Performance Evaluation**:

  - Continuously assess accuracy, reliability, and efficiency.

  - Example: A fraud detection system flagging significant drops in accuracy for human review.

- **Bias Detection and Mitigation**:

  - Identify and address biases emerging in real-time operations.

  - Example: A recommendation engine detecting demographic disparities in its output.

2. **Architectural Components**:

- **Monitoring Modules**:

  - Dedicated sub-systems for tracking compliance with ethical and operational standards.

- **Feedback Loops**:

  - Mechanisms to adjust algorithms or notify operators of detected issues.

  - Example: A healthcare AI system recalibrating its diagnostic models based on real-world outcomes.

- **Decision Logging**:

  - Maintain comprehensive logs for auditing and accountability.

  - Example: A credit scoring AI recording all factors influencing its decisions.

3. **Design Principles**:

- **Modularity**:
  - Create monitoring and self-regulation components that can be updated or replaced independently.
- **Explainability**:
  - Ensure that self-monitoring mechanisms provide clear and interpretable feedback.
- **Fail-Safes**:
  - Implement mechanisms to pause or shut down operations if self-monitoring detects critical violations.

. . . . . . . . . . . . . . . . . . . . . . . . . . . . . . . . .

*Adapting Systems to New Ethical Challenges*

As societal values, regulations, and technologies evolve, AI systems must adapt to remain ethically and operationally relevant.

1. **Dynamic Standards Integration**:
   - Enable systems to update their ethical frameworks based on new laws or guidelines.
   - Example: A privacy-focused chatbot adapting to changes in GDPR requirements.

2. **Real-Time Learning and Adjustment**:
   - Use machine learning techniques to refine system behavior based on new data and feedback.
   - Example: An autonomous vehicle learning to navigate new traffic laws introduced after deployment.

3. **Scenario Analysis and Simulation**:
   - Regularly test systems against hypothetical scenarios to evaluate their response to emerging ethical dilemmas.

- Example: A content moderation AI tested with new forms of hate speech.

4. **Collaboration with Stakeholders**:

- Engage ethicists, regulators, and end-users in updating systems to address evolving concerns.

- Example: Consulting mental health experts to refine an AI-powered therapy assistant.

• • • • • • • • • • • • • • • • • • • • • • • • • • • • • • • •

*Challenges in Implementing Recursive Monitoring and Self-Regulation*

While self-regulating systems offer significant advantages, they also present unique challenges that must be addressed.

1. **Technical Complexity**:

- Designing systems capable of real-time self-monitoring without impacting performance can be resource-intensive.

- Solution: Use lightweight monitoring algorithms optimized for efficiency.

2. **Interpretability**:

- Self-regulating mechanisms must provide actionable insights without overwhelming operators with technical jargon.

- Solution: Focus on creating interpretable outputs for diverse audiences.

3. **Data Dependency**:

- Recursive monitoring relies on continuous access to high-quality data, raising concerns about privacy and security.

- Solution: Use anonymized or synthetic data where possible.

4. **Cost and Maintenance:**

– Developing and maintaining self-regulating systems requires ongoing investment.

– Solution: Automate updates and leverage cloud-based solutions to reduce costs.

. . . . . . . . . . . . . . . . . . . . . . . . . . . . . . . . . . . .

*Benefits of Recursive Monitoring and Self-Regulation*
1. **Enhanced Accountability:**

– Continuous self-evaluation ensures that AI systems align with ethical guidelines even after deployment.

2. **Scalability:**

– Self-regulating systems reduce the need for constant human oversight, enabling scalability.

3. **Proactive Issue Resolution:**

– Systems can detect and address potential issues before they escalate into significant problems.

. . . . . . . . . . . . . . . . . . . . . . . . . . . . . . . . . . . .

*Checklist: Implementing Recursive Monitoring and Self-Regulation*
1. **Integrate Self-Regulation Modules During Design:**

– Develop monitoring components that track performance, compliance, and bias.

– Include real-time feedback loops and fail-safes in the architecture.

– Ensure modules are modular and upgradable.

2. **Conduct Regular System Updates for Evolving Ethical Standards:**

– Schedule periodic reviews to integrate new laws, guidelines, and user feedback.

– Use scenario-based testing to identify gaps in ethical

compliance.

3. **Validate Monitoring Outputs**:

-   Test the accuracy and reliability of self-monitoring mechanisms in real-world conditions.

-   Ensure outputs are interpretable for developers, users, and regulators.

4. **Involve Multidisciplinary Teams**:

-   Collaborate with ethicists, engineers, and legal experts to refine self-regulation mechanisms.

-   Example: Including cultural experts to ensure global relevance of ethical compliance.

5. **Implement Comprehensive Logging**:

-   Maintain detailed records of system behavior, decisions, and adjustments.

-   Use logs for auditing and to improve future system iterations.

6. **Audit Self-Regulation Modules Regularly**:

-   Partner with independent third parties to evaluate the effectiveness of monitoring systems.

-   Address identified issues promptly to maintain trust and compliance.

• • • • • • • • • • • • • • • • • • • • • • • • • • • • • • • •

*Conclusion*

Recursive monitoring and self-regulation enable AI systems to remain ethical, reliable, and adaptable in dynamic environments. By incorporating self-monitoring mechanisms during the design phase and regularly updating systems to reflect evolving standards, organizations can ensure long-term accountability and trustworthiness. This chapter provides a roadmap for building self-regulating AI systems, emphasizing the importance of proactive adaptation and multidisciplinary collaboration.

• • • • • • • • • • • • • • • • • • • • • • • • • • • • • • • • • • • • • • •

# CHAPTER 17: DEMOCRATIZING AI BENEFITS

*Introduction*

Artificial Intelligence (AI) has the potential to transform societies by solving complex problems, enhancing productivity, and improving quality of life. However, the benefits of AI are not distributed equitably, often exacerbating existing inequalities and creating a digital divide between those with access to advanced technologies and those without. Democratizing AI involves making AI accessible and beneficial to all, regardless of geography, socioeconomic status, or technical expertise. This chapter examines strategies to ensure equitable access to AI technologies, reduce the digital divide, and foster inclusion through open-source initiatives and accessible design.

*Ensuring Equitable Access to AI Technologies Globally*

Access to AI technologies varies widely across regions and demographics. Addressing this disparity requires targeted strategies to ensure inclusivity and fairness.

1. **Identifying Barriers to Access**:

   – **Economic Constraints**:

     • High costs of AI infrastructure, tools, and expertise limit adoption in underrepresented regions.

– **Lack of Infrastructure**:

- Limited access to high-speed internet, reliable electricity, and modern hardware in developing areas.

– **Educational Gaps**:

- Insufficient knowledge and training opportunities to understand and apply AI technologies.

– **Language Barriers**:

- AI tools predominantly cater to widely spoken languages, neglecting regional and indigenous languages.

2. **Strategies for Equitable Access**:

– **Affordability**:

- Develop cost-effective AI solutions for low-income communities.

- Example: Lightweight AI models that can run on low-power devices.

– **Localization**:

- Adapt AI tools for local languages, cultures, and contexts.

- Example: AI-powered translation tools supporting underrepresented languages.

– **Infrastructure Development**:

- Collaborate with governments and NGOs to improve digital infrastructure.

- Example: Internet access initiatives like Google's Project Loon or Starlink.

– **Education and Training**:

- Provide free or subsidized AI training programs in underserved areas.

- Example: Online courses and certification programs through platforms like Coursera or edX.

. . . . . . . . . . . . . . . . . . . . . . . . . . . . . . . . . . . . . .

*Reducing the Digital Divide Through Open-Source Initiatives*

Open-source AI initiatives play a critical role in democratizing access by providing free tools, resources, and platforms for innovation.

1. **Advantages of Open-Source AI**:

- **Cost Savings**:

- Eliminates licensing fees, making advanced technologies accessible to smaller organizations and individuals.

- **Collaboration and Innovation**:

- Encourages global collaboration to improve and customize tools for diverse applications.

- **Transparency**:

- Promotes trust by allowing users to examine and modify source code.

2. **Successful Open-Source AI Initiatives**:

- **TensorFlow**:

- A free and open-source library widely used for machine learning and AI development.

- **Hugging Face Transformers**:

- Open-source tools for natural language processing (NLP) supporting various languages and tasks.

- **OpenAI Gym**:

- A toolkit for developing and comparing

reinforcement learning algorithms.

3. **Challenges in Open-Source AI**:

– **Resource Requirements**:

- Some open-source projects still require advanced hardware and expertise.

– **Sustainability**:

- Maintaining and updating open-source projects can be challenging without consistent funding.

– **Misuse**:

- Open-source tools can be exploited for unethical purposes, such as creating harmful content.

4. **Solutions to Overcome Challenges**:

– **Provide Educational Resources**:

- Develop guides, tutorials, and examples to help users understand and apply open-source tools.

– **Secure Funding**:

- Encourage donations, sponsorships, and grants to sustain open-source communities.

– **Introduce Ethical Guidelines**:

- Establish and promote ethical usage policies for open-source AI tools.

• • • • • • • • • • • • • • • • • • • • • • • • • • • • • • • • •

*Prioritizing Accessibility in Design and Distribution*
To democratize AI, accessibility must be a priority during design and distribution.

1. **Inclusive Design Principles**:

– **Usability**:

- Simplify interfaces and workflows to make AI

tools intuitive for non-experts.

- Example: Drag-and-drop AI platforms like Google's AutoML.

– **Localization**:

- Adapt tools to support diverse languages, cultural nuances, and regional needs.

- Example: An AI agriculture app offering advice in multiple regional languages.

– **Accessibility Features**:

- Ensure tools are usable by individuals with disabilities.

- Example: Text-to-speech and screen reader compatibility for visually impaired users.

2. **Affordable Distribution Models**:

– **Freemium Models**:

- Offer basic AI services for free, with paid options for advanced features.

- Example: Cloud-based AI services like IBM Watson offering tiered pricing.

– **Partnerships with NGOs and Governments**:

- Collaborate to subsidize costs for deploying AI solutions in underserved communities.

3. **Case Studies of Accessible AI**:

– **Example 1: AI in Education**:

- Khan Academy's AI tutor provides personalized learning experiences for students worldwide.

– **Example 2: AI in Agriculture**:

- Apps like Plantix help small-scale farmers

diagnose crop diseases using smartphone cameras.

• • • • • • • • • • • • • • • • • • • • • • • • • • • • • • •

*Checklist: Democratizing AI Benefits*

1. **Develop Affordable AI Solutions for Underrepresented Groups**:

    – Create lightweight models that work on low-cost devices.

    – Offer subsidized or free access to essential AI tools and services.

2. **Prioritize Accessibility in Design and Distribution**:

    – Simplify user interfaces to make tools intuitive for non-experts.

    – Localize tools to support diverse languages and cultural contexts.

3. **Promote Open-Source AI Initiatives**:

    – Contribute to or create open-source AI tools that address global challenges.

    – Provide documentation and resources to help users adopt open-source technologies.

4. **Collaborate with Stakeholders**:

    – Partner with governments, NGOs, and private organizations to expand AI access.

    – Example: Joint ventures to improve digital infrastructure in rural areas.

5. **Invest in Education and Training**:

    – Offer free online courses, certifications, and training programs.

    – Establish AI learning hubs in underserved regions.

• • • • • • • • • • • • • • • • • • • • • • • • • • • • • • • • • •

*Conclusion*

Democratizing AI benefits is essential for bridging the digital divide and ensuring that the transformative power of AI reaches all of humanity. By making AI accessible, affordable, and inclusive, stakeholders can create a more equitable future where technology serves as a tool for empowerment rather than division. This chapter provides actionable strategies for developers, policymakers, and organizations to expand AI access, emphasizing the importance of open-source initiatives, inclusive design, and collaborative efforts.

• • • • • • • • • • • • • • • • • • • • • • • • • • • • • • • • • •

# CHAPTER 18:
# EDUCATING ETHICAL
# AI DEVELOPERS

• • • • • • • • • • • • • • • • • • • • • • • • • • • • • •

*Introduction*

The ethical challenges of artificial intelligence (AI) demand that developers not only master technical skills but also understand the broader societal, legal, and moral implications of their work. Integrating ethics into AI education ensures that future developers are equipped to create systems that prioritize fairness, accountability, and human well-being. This chapter provides comprehensive curriculum recommendations for embedding ethics into AI education, outlines training programs for interdisciplinary AI development, and includes actionable strategies to foster ethical expertise among developers.

• • • • • • • • • • • • • • • • • • • • • • • • • • • • • •

*Curriculum Recommendations for Embedding Ethics in Education*

AI education must evolve to incorporate ethical considerations alongside technical training. A robust curriculum ensures developers are prepared to address complex ethical dilemmas in real-world applications.

1. **Core Ethical Concepts**:

    –        Introduce foundational ethical theories and their relevance to AI.

        •        **Utilitarianism**: Maximizing benefits while

minimizing harm.

- **Deontology**: Adhering to rules and principles regardless of outcomes.

- **Virtue Ethics**: Fostering moral character in decision-making.

2. **AI-Specific Ethical Topics**:

– **Bias and Fairness**:

- Understanding how bias arises in datasets and algorithms.

- Techniques to detect and mitigate bias in AI systems.

– **Transparency and Explainability**:

- Importance of making AI decisions understandable to users.

- Tools and techniques for improving explainability.

– **Accountability**:

- Assigning responsibility for AI decisions and outcomes.

– **Privacy and Security**:

- Ethical handling of user data and compliance with regulations like GDPR.

3. **Case Studies and Real-World Applications**:

– Analyze examples of ethical successes and failures in AI.

– Example: The misuse of AI in facial recognition technology and its societal impact.

4. **Practical Training in Ethical AI Development**:

– Implement hands-on projects that challenge students

to design ethically compliant systems.

–    Example: Developing an AI model for hiring that ensures fairness across demographics.

5.   **Interdisciplinary Perspectives**:

–    Incorporate insights from fields like sociology, law, psychology, and philosophy to broaden understanding of AI's societal impact.

• • • • • • • • • • • • • • • • • • • • • • • • • • • • • • • • • •

*Training Programs for Interdisciplinary AI Development*
To address the multifaceted nature of AI ethics, training programs must encourage collaboration across disciplines and sectors.

1.   **Interdisciplinary Courses**:

–    Combine AI ethics with technical subjects, legal studies, and social sciences.

–    Example: A course exploring the intersection of AI, privacy laws, and user rights.

2.   **Workshops and Bootcamps**:

–    Short-term intensive programs focused on specific ethical topics.

–    Example: A weekend workshop on detecting and mitigating bias in machine learning.

3.   **Corporate Training Programs**:

–    Tailor ethics training for professionals in AI-related roles.

–    Example: Training sessions on ethical considerations in product lifecycle management.

4.   **Collaboration with Academic Institutions**:

–    Partner with universities to integrate ethical

AI modules into computer science and engineering programs.

- Example: A joint initiative between a tech company and a university to develop a specialized AI ethics curriculum.

5. **Multidisciplinary Team Projects**:

- Encourage teams of developers, ethicists, and sociologists to work on AI projects.

- Example: A team designing a chatbot for mental health support, balancing technical feasibility and ethical considerations.

• • • • • • • • • • • • • • • • • • • • • • • • • • • • • • • • • • •

*Role of Certifications in Ethical AI Development*

Certifications provide a standardized way to ensure professionals are equipped with the knowledge and skills to develop ethical AI.

1. **Benefits of Certification Programs**:

- Validate expertise in ethical AI practices.

- Enhance credibility and employability of developers.

- Promote standardized approaches to AI ethics.

2. **Components of Certification Programs**:

- **Core Curriculum**:

    • Ethical theories, bias mitigation, transparency, and accountability.

- **Practical Assessments**:

    • Case studies and real-world problem-solving exercises.

- **Continuous Learning**:

    • Periodic updates to certification content to reflect

evolving ethical challenges.

3. **Examples of Existing Certifications:**

–    **MIT AI Ethics and Governance Program**: Offers training on ethical implications of AI in governance.

–    **AI4ALL Open Learning**: Focuses on inclusive and ethical AI development.

4. **Industry Recognition:**

–    Collaborate with professional organizations to ensure certifications are widely recognized and respected.

• • • • • • • • • • • • • • • • • • • • • • • • • • • • • • • • • • •

*Checklist: Educating Ethical AI Developers*

1. **Partner with Academic Institutions for Ethics Training:**

–    Collaborate with universities to design and deliver ethics-integrated AI programs.

–    Example: Co-developing a course on AI ethics with a university's computer science department.

2. **Offer Certification Programs in Ethical AI Development:**

–    Create certifications that validate ethical expertise for developers.

–    Partner with industry leaders to promote certification adoption.

3. **Incorporate Case Studies and Practical Training:**

–    Use real-world examples to teach ethical principles and decision-making.

–    Example: Assigning students to analyze and propose solutions for historical AI failures.

4. **Encourage Interdisciplinary Collaboration:**

- Organize team projects involving developers, ethicists, sociologists, and legal experts.

- Example: A capstone project requiring students to design an AI system for equitable resource allocation.

5. **Promote Lifelong Learning**:

- Provide resources for professionals to stay updated on evolving ethical challenges.

- Example: Online courses, webinars, and forums for ethical AI discussions.

6. **Engage Industry Leaders in Training**:

- Invite guest lecturers and practitioners to share insights on real-world applications of ethical AI.

- Example: A tech company CEO discussing lessons learned from deploying ethical AI solutions.

• • • • • • • • • • • • • • • • • • • • • • • • • • • • • • • • • • •

*Conclusion*

Educating ethical AI developers is a cornerstone of responsible AI innovation. By embedding ethics into curricula, fostering interdisciplinary collaboration, and offering certification programs, we can equip future developers with the skills and knowledge to create technology that serves humanity ethically and equitably. This chapter provides actionable strategies for integrating ethics into AI education, ensuring a future where AI development aligns with societal values and moral imperatives.

• • • • • • • • • • • • • • • • • • • • • • • • • • • • • • • • • • •

# CHAPTER 19:
# TOOLKITS FOR
# ETHICAL AI

. . . . . . . . . . . . . . . . . . . . . . . . . . . . . . . . .

*Introduction*

The complexities of developing ethical AI demand practical tools that assist developers, organizations, and policymakers in identifying and addressing ethical risks throughout the AI lifecycle. Toolkits, frameworks, and scoring systems offer systematic approaches to evaluate and improve fairness, transparency, accountability, and compliance with ethical standards. This chapter explores available resources for ethical AI evaluation, highlights open-source tools for bias testing and explainability, and provides actionable strategies to integrate these tools into development pipelines.

. . . . . . . . . . . . . . . . . . . . . . . . . . . . . . . . .

*Checklists, Scoring Systems, and Frameworks*
*for Ethical Evaluations*

Comprehensive tools are essential for embedding ethics into the AI development process. Checklists, scoring systems, and frameworks enable consistent evaluation and accountability across teams and projects.

1. **Checklists for Ethical AI Development**:

    – Structured lists to ensure ethical considerations are addressed at every stage.

- **Examples:**

  - **Google's Responsible AI Guidelines**: Covers privacy, fairness, and inclusivity in AI systems.

  - **AI Ethics Checklist**: Evaluates transparency, accountability, and safety.

2. **Scoring Systems:**

- Quantitative metrics to assess ethical compliance and identify areas for improvement.

- **Examples:**

  - **AI Fairness Score**: Measures demographic parity and equal opportunity in decision-making systems.

  - **Ethical Maturity Model**: Rates organizations on their adherence to ethical practices.

- **Benefits:**

  - Standardized assessments allow for benchmarking across projects.

  - Scoring highlights specific areas requiring intervention.

3. **Frameworks for Ethical AI:**

- Holistic approaches to embedding ethics into AI systems, combining checklists, metrics, and methodologies.

- **Examples:**

  - **Microsoft's AI Ethics Principles Framework:**

    - Focuses on fairness, inclusiveness, reliability, transparency, privacy, and accountability.

  - **PWC Responsible AI Toolkit:**

    - Includes diagnostic tools, action plans, and

monitoring mechanisms.

4. **Use Case**:

– **Example**: A financial institution using an ethical AI checklist to audit its credit scoring system, ensuring compliance with anti-discrimination laws.

• • • • • • • • • • • • • • • • • • • • • • • • • • • • • • • • • • •

*Open-Source Tools for Bias Testing, Fairness Assessment, and Explainability*

Open-source tools provide accessible and customizable resources for developers and organizations to evaluate and improve AI systems.

1. **Bias Detection and Fairness Assessment Tools**:

– **AI Fairness 360 (AIF360)**:

• Developed by IBM, it provides a comprehensive library for detecting and mitigating bias in datasets and machine learning models.

• Features:

– Pre-processing, in-processing, and post-processing bias mitigation algorithms.

– Visualization tools for fairness metrics.

– **Fairlearn**:

• An open-source toolkit by Microsoft for assessing and improving fairness in AI models.

• Features:

– Fairness metrics and visualization dashboards.

– Algorithms to mitigate unfair treatment of specific groups.

– **WEKA**:

- A machine learning toolkit with bias detection and fairness evaluation capabilities.

- Features:

  - Supports fairness-aware machine learning workflows.

2. **Explainability Tools:**

- **LIME (Local Interpretable Model-Agnostic Explanations):**

  - Explains individual predictions by approximating complex models with interpretable ones.

- **SHAP (SHapley Additive exPlanations):**

  - Assigns importance values to features influencing model predictions.

- **What-If Tool:**

  - An interactive visualization tool by Google for exploring AI model predictions and their fairness.

3. **General-Purpose Ethical AI Toolkits:**

- **Ethical Explorer Pack:**

  - A toolkit for identifying ethical risks in AI projects and brainstorming solutions.

- **TensorFlow Responsible AI Toolkit:**

  - Offers pre-trained models and guidelines for building fair and transparent AI systems.

4. **Use Case:**

- **Example:** A healthcare provider using AI Fairness 360 to detect bias in patient diagnosis models and SHAP to explain decisions to medical professionals.

· · · · · · · · · · · · · · · · · · · · · · · · · · · · · · · · · · ·

*Integrating Toolkits into Development Pipelines*

To maximize the impact of ethical AI toolkits, they must be seamlessly integrated into existing development workflows.

1. **Establish Ethical Evaluation as a Standard Phase:**

   - Include ethical evaluations in each stage of the AI lifecycle: data collection, model training, deployment, and monitoring.

2. **Automate Bias and Fairness Testing:**

   - Integrate tools like AIF360 or Fairlearn into Continuous Integration/Continuous Deployment (CI/CD) pipelines.

   - Example: Automatically flagging datasets or models exhibiting bias during regular builds.

3. **Encourage Collaboration:**

   - Train teams to use ethical toolkits effectively.

   - Foster collaboration between developers, ethicists, and end-users to interpret findings and implement changes.

4. **Track Progress with Scoring Systems:**

   - Use scoring systems to monitor improvements over time and benchmark against industry standards.

   - Example: Assigning fairness scores to models and tracking their evolution with updates.

• • • • • • • • • • • • • • • • • • • • • • • • • • • • • • • • • •

*Checklist: Using Toolkits for Ethical AI Development*

1. **Integrate Bias-Detection Tools into Development Pipelines:**

   - Use tools like AI Fairness 360 or Fairlearn to identify and mitigate biases in datasets and models.

   - Automate regular testing for fairness during development.

2. **Use Scoring Systems to Evaluate Ethical Compliance**:

   – Adopt scoring systems to measure adherence to ethical guidelines.

   – Example: Generate quarterly ethical compliance reports using metrics from tools like AIF360.

3. **Incorporate Explainability Tools**:

   – Leverage tools like LIME, SHAP, or the What-If Tool to make AI decisions transparent and interpretable.

   – Regularly test explainability outputs for accuracy and usability.

4. **Establish Documentation Standards**:

   – Document all findings, actions, and decisions related to ethical evaluations.

   – Example: Maintain detailed logs of bias mitigation efforts for accountability.

5. **Train Teams on Toolkit Usage**:

   – Provide regular training sessions to ensure developers understand and can effectively use ethical AI tools.

   – Example: Organize workshops on integrating AI Fairness 360 into data pipelines.

6. **Monitor and Update Toolkits**:

   – Regularly evaluate and update toolkits to incorporate new features, metrics, and best practices.

   – Example: Periodically review open-source updates and incorporate them into workflows.

• • • • • • • • • • • • • • • • • • • • • • • • • • • • • • • • • • • •

*Conclusion*

Toolkits for ethical AI provide practical resources for identifying, evaluating, and mitigating risks throughout the AI lifecycle. By integrating these tools into development pipelines and leveraging open-source solutions, organizations can ensure fairness, transparency, and accountability in their AI systems. This chapter outlines actionable strategies to use checklists, scoring systems, and frameworks effectively, empowering developers and organizations to achieve ethical excellence in AI innovation.

• • • • • • • • • • • • • • • • • • • • • • • • • • • • • • • • • • •

# CHAPTER 20: IMPLEMENTING ETHICAL AI IN INDUSTRY

• • • • • • • • • • • • • • • • • • • • • • • • • • • • • • •

*Introduction*

The adoption of ethical AI in industry is critical to ensuring that advanced technologies benefit society while minimizing risks. As AI becomes a cornerstone of various sectors—healthcare, finance, manufacturing, and more—each industry faces unique ethical challenges. This chapter provides comprehensive industry-specific guidelines for deploying ethical AI, emphasizes the importance of collaboration between corporations, governments, and NGOs, and outlines actionable strategies to ensure compliance and accountability.

• • • • • • • • • • • • • • • • • • • • • • • • • • • • • • •

*Industry-Specific Guidelines for Deploying Ethical AI*

Each industry has distinct ethical concerns and operational requirements. Below are tailored guidelines for key sectors:

1. **Healthcare**:

   – **Ethical Challenges**:

      • Ensuring unbiased diagnostic tools.

      • Protecting patient privacy under regulations like

HIPAA and GDPR.

- **Best Practices**:

    - Use diverse datasets to avoid demographic bias in AI-powered diagnostic tools.

    - Design systems with explainability features to assist healthcare professionals in decision-making.

    - Regularly audit models for compliance with patient privacy laws.

- **Example**: Deploying AI for early cancer detection with clear documentation of decision pathways for physicians.

2. **Finance**:

- **Ethical Challenges**:

    - Preventing algorithmic bias in lending decisions.

    - Safeguarding against fraud and data breaches.

- **Best Practices**:

    - Incorporate fairness metrics in credit scoring systems to ensure equal access to loans.

    - Use anomaly detection algorithms to enhance fraud prevention while respecting user privacy.

- **Example**: A bank using AI to assess loan applications but requiring human oversight for high-risk cases.

3. **Manufacturing**:

- **Ethical Challenges**:

    - Worker displacement due to automation.

    - Ensuring safety in AI-powered machinery.

- **Best Practices**:

    - Provide retraining programs for workers impacted

by automation.

- Implement fail-safes in robotics to prevent workplace accidents.

– **Example**: Automating assembly lines while reskilling employees for supervisory roles.

4. **Retail and E-Commerce**:

– **Ethical Challenges**:

- Avoiding manipulative practices in targeted advertising.

- Ensuring transparency in AI-driven recommendations.

– **Best Practices**:

- Use algorithms that prioritize user benefit over maximizing profits.

- Clearly label sponsored content and personalized recommendations.

– **Example**: An e-commerce platform providing explanations for why certain products are recommended.

5. **Public Sector and Government**:

– **Ethical Challenges**:

- Avoiding misuse of surveillance technologies.

- Ensuring transparency and accountability in public services.

– **Best Practices**:

- Limit the use of facial recognition technologies to cases with strong oversight and clear regulations.

- Use explainable AI in decision-making systems for public services to build trust with citizens.

– **Example**: A city government using AI for traffic management while anonymizing collected data.

· · · · · · · · · · · · · · · · · · · · · · · · · · · · · · · · · · · ·

*Collaboration Between Corporations, Governments, and NGOs*

Deploying ethical AI at scale requires coordinated efforts across multiple stakeholders.

1. **Corporations**:

– **Role**:

  • Develop and deploy AI technologies with built-in ethical safeguards.

  • Set industry standards through self-regulation and innovation.

– **Examples of Action**:

  • Tech companies adopting responsible AI principles, such as Microsoft's AI ethics framework.

2. **Governments**:

– **Role**:

  • Establish regulatory frameworks and enforce compliance.

  • Fund research and development for ethical AI initiatives.

– **Examples of Action**:

  • Governments introducing AI-specific laws, such as the EU's Artificial Intelligence Act.

3. **Non-Governmental Organizations (NGOs)**:

– **Role**:

  • Advocate for public interests and provide independent oversight.

- Raise awareness about ethical challenges in AI.

   – **Examples of Action**:

- NGOs like the Partnership on AI promoting transparency and fairness in AI development.

4. **Collaboration Mechanisms**:

   – **Public-Private Partnerships**:

- Joint ventures between corporations and governments to address ethical challenges.

- Example: Collaborating on AI solutions for healthcare while ensuring patient privacy.

   – **Multi-Stakeholder Platforms**:

- Forums where corporations, governments, NGOs, and academics discuss ethical concerns and solutions.

- Example: Global initiatives like the AI for Good Summit by the United Nations.

• • • • • • • • • • • • • • • • • • • • • • • • • • • • • • • • • •

*Strategies for Industry-Wide Ethical AI Implementation*

1. **Establish Ethical Policies**:

   – Develop clear, industry-specific guidelines for ethical AI practices.

   – Example: A financial institution adopting policies to ensure fairness in lending algorithms.

2. **Create Ethical Oversight Committees**:

   – Form internal committees to review AI projects for ethical compliance.

   – Include diverse stakeholders, including ethicists, engineers, and end-users.

3. **Perform Regular Audits**:

– Conduct periodic evaluations of AI systems to ensure adherence to ethical standards.

– Partner with third-party auditors for unbiased reviews.

– Example: A retail company auditing its recommendation algorithms to detect hidden biases.

4. **Train Employees on Ethical AI**:

– Provide training programs for employees to understand and apply ethical AI principles.

– Example: A tech company offering workshops on bias detection in machine learning.

5. **Monitor Post-Deployment Impact**:

– Continuously assess the societal and environmental impact of deployed AI systems.

– Use user feedback to refine and improve systems.

· · · · · · · · · · · · · · · · · · · · · · · · · · · · · · · · · · · · · · · ·

*Checklist: Implementing Ethical AI in Industry*

1. **Create Industry-Specific Ethical Policies**:

– Define ethical standards tailored to your industry's unique challenges.

– Collaborate with stakeholders to align policies with global best practices.

2. **Perform Regular Reviews of Deployed Systems for Compliance**:

– Schedule periodic audits to evaluate AI systems for fairness, transparency, and accountability.

– Document audit results and use findings to improve systems.

3. **Foster Multi-Stakeholder Collaboration**:

– Partner with governments, NGOs, and other industry

players to create unified ethical guidelines.

–    Example: Participate in initiatives like the Global Partnership on Artificial Intelligence (GPAI).

4.  **Establish Ethical Oversight Committees**:

–    Form internal committees to evaluate AI projects during design, deployment, and post-deployment phases.

–    Include representatives from diverse disciplines and user groups.

5.  **Invest in Employee Training**:

–    Offer ethics training programs to ensure all employees understand their role in ethical AI development.

–    Example: Regularly update training content to reflect evolving standards.

6.  **Ensure Transparency with Stakeholders**:

–    Communicate clearly about the capabilities, limitations, and ethical safeguards of AI systems.

–    Example: Publicly disclose the use of AI in decision-making processes.

* * *

*Conclusion*

Implementing ethical AI in industry requires a collaborative, multi-faceted approach that addresses the specific challenges of each sector. By establishing industry-specific policies, fostering partnerships with governments and NGOs, and prioritizing transparency and accountability, organizations can ensure that AI technologies are deployed responsibly. This chapter provides a roadmap for embedding ethics into industrial AI practices, empowering businesses to leverage AI for societal good while maintaining public trust.

# CHAPTER 21: THE ETHICAL AI ROADMAP

●●●●●●●●●●●●●●●●●●●●●●●●●●●●●●●●●●●●●

*Introduction*

As AI continues to transform industries and societies, organizations must create comprehensive roadmaps to ensure the long-term ethical development and deployment of AI systems. An Ethical AI Roadmap provides a structured approach for embedding ethics into the entire lifecycle of AI technologies, from inception to post-deployment. This chapter outlines the key elements of building such a roadmap, including defining Key Performance Indicators (KPIs) and success metrics to track compliance and progress.

●●●●●●●●●●●●●●●●●●●●●●●●●●●●●●●●●●●●●

*Creating a Roadmap for Long-Term Ethical AI Development*

An Ethical AI Roadmap serves as a strategic guide for aligning AI initiatives with organizational values, societal expectations, and regulatory requirements.

1. **Define Ethical AI Objectives**:

   – Clearly articulate the organization's vision and goals for ethical AI.

   – Example: "Our AI systems will prioritize fairness, transparency, and user privacy."

2. **Establish Guiding Principles**:

   – Base principles on core ethical values such as fairness, accountability, transparency, and inclusivity.

- Example: Incorporate globally recognized frameworks like the OECD AI Principles.

3. **Develop an Ethical AI Governance Structure**:

- Appoint a Chief Ethics Officer or equivalent role to oversee ethical AI initiatives.

- Create cross-functional committees including ethicists, engineers, and user representatives.

4. **Integrate Ethics into the AI Development Lifecycle**:

- Embed ethical considerations into every stage of development:

  - **Data Collection**: Ensure data privacy, consent, and representativeness.

  - **Model Training**: Mitigate biases and prioritize fairness.

  - **Deployment**: Implement explainability, accountability, and safety mechanisms.

  - **Monitoring**: Continuously assess ethical performance post-deployment.

5. **Align with Regulatory and Industry Standards**:

- Stay updated on legal requirements and industry best practices.

- Example: Adhere to regulations like GDPR for data protection and the EU AI Act for AI compliance.

• • • • • • • • • • • • • • • • • • • • • • • • • • • • • • • • • • • • •

*Defining KPIs and Success Metrics for Ethical Compliance*

Key Performance Indicators (KPIs) and success metrics are essential for measuring the effectiveness of ethical AI initiatives. These metrics help organizations track progress, identify areas for improvement, and ensure accountability.

1. **Categories of Ethical AI KPIs**:

- **Fairness:**

  - Measure disparities in outcomes across demographic groups.

  - Example: Disparate Impact Ratio for evaluating fairness in hiring algorithms.

- **Transparency:**

  - Track the percentage of systems with explainability features implemented.

  - Example: Proportion of models providing clear and interpretable outputs.

- **Privacy and Security:**

  - Monitor compliance with data protection regulations and the number of privacy breaches.

  - Example: Number of systems employing end-to-end encryption.

- **User Trust and Satisfaction:**

  - Gather feedback from users on perceived fairness, accuracy, and usability.

  - Example: Net Promoter Score (NPS) for AI systems.

- **Bias Detection and Mitigation:**

  - Evaluate the effectiveness of bias mitigation efforts.

  - Example: Percentage reduction in model bias after retraining.

2. **Setting Targets for KPIs:**

- Define achievable and meaningful benchmarks for each KPI.

- Example: "Achieve a Disparate Impact Ratio of 0.8 or higher for all decision-making systems."

3. **Regular KPI Tracking and Reporting**:
- Establish processes for monitoring KPIs at regular intervals.
- Use dashboards and reports to communicate progress to stakeholders.

4. **Case Study: KPI Implementation**:
- **Scenario**: A financial institution tracks bias mitigation and fairness in its loan approval AI.
- **KPIs**:
  - Percentage of applications flagged for bias review.
  - Average approval rate disparity between demographic groups.
- **Results**: A 15% improvement in fairness metrics after retraining the model.

• • • • • • • • • • • • • • • • • • • • • • • • • • • • • • • • • •

*Checklist: Building and Maintaining an Ethical AI Roadmap*
1. **Publish Organizational AI Ethics Policies**:
- Clearly articulate ethical principles and commitments.
- Example: A public statement on prioritizing fairness and transparency in AI applications.

2. **Establish Governance Structures**:
- Appoint an ethics officer or create a committee responsible for ethical oversight.
- Define roles and responsibilities for ethical compliance.

3. **Track KPIs Regularly to Ensure Ethical Success**:
- Implement tracking mechanisms for fairness, transparency, and other KPIs.
- Use data visualization tools to monitor progress and

identify gaps.

4. **Engage Stakeholders**:

– Involve users, policymakers, and industry experts in defining ethical priorities.

– Conduct regular feedback sessions to refine the roadmap.

5. **Align with Evolving Standards**:

– Update the roadmap to reflect changes in regulations, societal expectations, and technological advancements.

6. **Conduct Regular Audits**:

– Partner with independent auditors to review adherence to ethical policies.

– Use audit findings to improve the roadmap and practices.

7. **Foster a Culture of Ethical Awareness**:

– Train employees on the importance of ethical AI and how to achieve it.

– Example: Regular workshops and seminars on emerging ethical issues.

• • • • • • • • • • • • • • • • • • • • • • • • • • • • • • • • • • • •

*Conclusion*

The Ethical AI Roadmap is a dynamic framework that enables organizations to integrate ethical principles into every aspect of AI development and deployment. By defining clear objectives, tracking meaningful KPIs, and engaging stakeholders, organizations can ensure their AI systems align with societal values and regulatory standards. This chapter provides a step-by-step guide for creating and maintaining an Ethical AI Roadmap, empowering organizations to achieve long-term ethical success.

# CONCLUSION: SHAPING THE FUTURE OF AI

*Reflecting on the Challenges and Opportunities of Ethical AI*

The development of artificial intelligence represents one of humanity's most transformative endeavors, with the potential to revolutionize industries, solve global challenges, and enhance daily life. However, as with any powerful tool, AI also brings significant ethical challenges. The rapid evolution of AI systems has exposed vulnerabilities in societal, legal, and moral frameworks, including biases in algorithms, privacy concerns, and the potential misuse of autonomous technologies.

**Key Challenges:**

1. **Bias and Discrimination**:

   – AI systems have inadvertently perpetuated societal inequalities due to biased training data and flawed design.

   – Example: Disparities in hiring algorithms or facial recognition systems disproportionately impacting marginalized groups.

2. **Transparency and Accountability**:

   – The "black-box" nature of some AI models undermines trust, as users and regulators cannot easily understand or scrutinize decisions.

3. **Global Inequities**:

- The benefits of AI remain unevenly distributed, with developed nations reaping the most rewards while others face barriers to access.

4. **Weaponization and Misuse**:

- The potential for AI to be weaponized in warfare or used for malicious purposes raises profound ethical concerns.

5. **Erosion of Privacy**:

- AI-driven surveillance systems and data exploitation threaten personal freedoms and privacy.

Despite these challenges, the opportunities presented by ethical AI are vast:

- **Advancing Medicine**: AI can revolutionize diagnostics, treatment planning, and healthcare delivery.

- **Sustainable Development**: AI-driven solutions can optimize resource use, combat climate change, and enhance agricultural productivity.

- **Education and Empowerment**: Personalized learning platforms powered by AI can bridge educational gaps and foster lifelong learning.

. . . . . . . . . . . . . . . . . . . . . . . . . . . . . . . . . . .

*A Call to Action for a United Global Effort*
*in Ethical AI Development*

To harness AI's potential while safeguarding against its risks, a unified global effort is essential. No single organization or country can address these challenges alone. Ethical AI requires collaboration across industries, governments, academia, and civil society.

1. **Governments and Policymakers**:

- Implement regulations that protect against AI misuse

while encouraging innovation.

– Example: Policies such as the European Union's Artificial Intelligence Act, which balances safety with technological advancement.

2. **Corporations and Developers**:

– Adopt transparent development practices and commit to ethical principles.

– Example: Companies integrating explainability and fairness into their product design pipelines.

3. **Academic and Research Institutions**:

– Lead in interdisciplinary research that combines technical innovation with ethical inquiry.

– Example: Universities establishing AI ethics programs and contributing to open-source ethical toolkits.

4. **Non-Governmental Organizations (NGOs)**:

– Advocate for vulnerable populations, ensuring AI systems are inclusive and equitable.

– Example: NGOs monitoring the ethical deployment of AI in developing regions.

5. **Global Coalitions**:

– Foster international collaboration to set universal ethical standards and share best practices.

– Example: The Global Partnership on Artificial Intelligence (GPAI) promoting responsible AI use worldwide.

• • • • • • • • • • • • • • • • • • • • • • • • • • • • • • •

*Inspiring a Vision of AI as a Force for Universal Good*

As we shape the future of AI, we must strive to make it a force for universal good—a technology that transcends boundaries, fosters equity, and enhances the human experience. By addressing ethical challenges head-on and embedding ethics into every stage of AI development, we can realize its transformative potential responsibly.

**A Vision for AI's Future:**

1. **Empowering Humanity:**

   – AI should augment human capabilities, enabling individuals to reach their full potential.

   – Example: AI-powered tools simplifying complex tasks, freeing people to focus on creativity and innovation.

2. **Fostering Inclusivity:**

   – Ensure that AI systems reflect the diversity of global populations, providing equitable benefits to all.

   – Example: Multilingual AI platforms that break down language barriers.

3. **Driving Sustainability:**

   – Leverage AI for solutions that protect the planet and promote sustainable living.

   – Example: AI optimizing renewable energy grids and reducing carbon emissions.

4. **Promoting Peace and Collaboration:**

   – Use AI to build bridges between communities and address shared global challenges.

   – Example: AI systems fostering dialogue in conflict resolution or managing humanitarian aid distribution.

5. **Preserving Human Dignity and Autonomy:**

   – Ensure that AI systems respect individual rights and freedoms, never replacing human judgment in critical decisions.

   – Example: Transparent AI systems in judicial and

healthcare applications.

· · · · · · · · · · · · · · · · · · · · · · · · · · · · · · · · · ·

*A Shared Responsibility*

The future of AI is a shared responsibility, requiring commitment from all sectors of society. The Ethical AI Bible, as presented in this work, is a foundational step toward guiding humanity in navigating this transformative era. Its principles, tools, and frameworks are designed not only to address today's challenges but also to anticipate and adapt to tomorrow's.

· · · · · · · · · · · · · · · · · · · · · · · · · · · · · · · · · ·

*A Final Thought*

AI's story is ultimately a reflection of our collective choices. By prioritizing ethics, inclusivity, and sustainability, we can write a story of progress and hope—one where AI becomes not just a tool, but a partner in shaping a better, fairer, and more compassionate world. Together, we can ensure that AI serves as a beacon of human ingenuity and moral responsibility, illuminating the path to a future where technology uplifts and unites all of humanity.

· · · · · · · · · · · · · · · · · · · · · · · · · · · · · · · · · ·

# APPENDIX A:
# GLOSSARY OF TERMS

This glossary provides definitions and explanations for key terms and concepts used throughout the book. It serves as a quick reference for readers seeking to understand the terminology relevant to ethical AI development and deployment.

**A**

- **Algorithm**: A set of rules or instructions a computer follows to solve problems or make decisions.

- **Artificial Intelligence (AI)**: The simulation of human intelligence in machines programmed to perform tasks that typically require human cognition, such as learning, reasoning, and decision-making.

- **Autonomous Systems**: Systems capable of operating without human intervention, such as self-driving cars or drones.

**B**

- **Bias**: A tendency of an AI system to produce results that are systematically unfair or favor certain groups due to flaws in data or design.

- **Black-Box Model**: An AI model whose internal workings are not easily interpretable, making it difficult to understand how decisions are made.

- **Blockchain**: A decentralized ledger technology used for recording transactions securely and transparently.

• • • • • • • • • • • • • • • • • • • • • • • • • • • • • • • • •

C

- **Compliance**: Adherence to laws, regulations, or ethical guidelines.

- **Consent**: The voluntary agreement of an individual to allow their data to be collected or used for specific purposes.

- **Continuous Monitoring**: The process of continuously assessing an AI system's performance, compliance, and ethical impact after deployment.

• • • • • • • • • • • • • • • • • • • • • • • • • • • • • • • • •

D

- **Data Anonymization**: The process of removing personally identifiable information from data to protect individual privacy.

- **Deep Learning**: A subset of machine learning that uses neural networks with multiple layers to analyze complex patterns in data.

- **Disparate Impact**: A situation where an AI system adversely affects a particular group, even without intentional discrimination.

• • • • • • • • • • • • • • • • • • • • • • • • • • • • • • • • •

E

- **Ethical AI**: The development and deployment of AI systems that align with moral principles such as fairness, transparency, and accountability.

- **Explainability**: The ability to understand and interpret the decisions or outputs of an AI system.

- **Encryption**: A method of securing data by converting it into a code to prevent unauthorized access.

. . . . . . . . . . . . . . . . . . . . . . . . . . . . . . . . . . .

**F**

- **Fairness**: The principle that AI systems should produce equitable outcomes and avoid discrimination against any individual or group.

- **Feedback Loop**: A system in which outputs are fed back as inputs, allowing for continuous learning and adaptation.

- **Fail-Safe**: A mechanism designed to prevent harm by shutting down or reverting an AI system to a safe state when errors occur.

. . . . . . . . . . . . . . . . . . . . . . . . . . . . . . . . . . .

**G**

- **General Data Protection Regulation (GDPR)**: A European Union regulation governing data protection and privacy for individuals.

- **Governance**: The frameworks, policies, and practices used to manage and regulate AI systems.

. . . . . . . . . . . . . . . . . . . . . . . . . . . . . . . . . . .

**H**

- **Human-in-the-Loop (HITL)**: A model where humans are involved in the decision-making process of an AI system to ensure oversight and control.

- **Hyperparameter Tuning**: The process of optimizing the parameters of a machine learning model to improve performance.

. . . . . . . . . . . . . . . . . . . . . . . . . . . . . . . . . . .

**I**

- **Interdisciplinary AI Development**: The collaboration of experts from various fields—such as computer science, ethics, sociology, and law—in the design and deployment of AI systems.

- **Interpretability**: The degree to which a human can understand the reasons behind a model's output.

• • • • • • • • • • • • • • • • • • • • • • • • • • • • •

**K**

- **Key Performance Indicator (KPI)**: A measurable value that indicates how effectively an AI system achieves specific objectives, such as fairness or accuracy.

- **Kill Switch**: A mechanism to immediately deactivate an AI system in the event of malfunction or misuse.

• • • • • • • • • • • • • • • • • • • • • • • • • • • • •

**L**

- **Machine Learning (ML)**: A subset of AI that allows systems to learn from data and improve performance without explicit programming.

- **Metadata**: Data that provides information about other data, such as creation date or source.

• • • • • • • • • • • • • • • • • • • • • • • • • • • • •

**N**

- **Neural Network**: A computational model inspired by the human brain, used in machine learning to recognize patterns and make predictions.

- **Non-Governmental Organization (NGO)**: An organization independent of governments, often focused on advocacy or humanitarian work.

• • • • • • • • • • • • • • • • • • • • • • • • • • • • •

**O**

- **Open Source**: Software or tools whose source code is publicly available, allowing anyone to use, modify, or distribute it.

. . . . . . . . . . . . . . . . . . . . . . . . . . . . . . . . . . . .

## P

- **Privacy by Design**: An approach to system development that incorporates data privacy and protection principles from the outset.

- **Predictive Analytics**: The use of statistical techniques and algorithms to forecast future outcomes based on historical data.

. . . . . . . . . . . . . . . . . . . . . . . . . . . . . . . . . . . .

## R

- **Recursive Monitoring**: The continuous self-assessment of an AI system to ensure ethical compliance and operational reliability.

- **Reinforcement Learning**: A machine learning approach where agents learn by receiving rewards or penalties for their actions.

. . . . . . . . . . . . . . . . . . . . . . . . . . . . . . . . . . . .

## S

- **Scoring System**: A framework for evaluating the ethical performance of an AI system using predefined metrics.

- **Self-Regulation**: The ability of an AI system to monitor and adjust its operations to maintain ethical compliance.

- **Sustainability**: The principle of designing AI systems to minimize environmental and societal impacts.

. . . . . . . . . . . . . . . . . . . . . . . . . . . . . . . . . . . .

## T

- **Transparency**: The openness of an AI system, allowing stakeholders to understand its processes, decisions, and limitations.

- **Trustworthiness**: The degree to which users can rely on an AI system to operate safely, ethically, and effectively.

**U**

- **Unsupervised Learning**: A type of machine learning where algorithms identify patterns in data without labeled examples.

- **Universal Principles of AI Ethics**: Fundamental guidelines, such as fairness, accountability, and transparency, applicable to AI systems worldwide.

**V**

- **Virtue Ethics**: An ethical framework emphasizing moral character and virtues, applied to the behavior of AI systems and their developers.

**W**

- **Watermarking**: Embedding identifying markers into AI-generated content to verify authenticity and origin.

- **Whistleblower Protection**: Safeguards for individuals reporting unethical practices in AI development or deployment.

**X**

- **Explainable AI (XAI)**: AI systems designed to provide clear, interpretable explanations for their decisions and outputs.

**Z**

- **Zero-Day Vulnerability**: A security flaw that is unknown to those responsible for fixing it, making it a significant risk in AI systems.

This glossary offers a foundational understanding of essential

AI and ethics-related terminology, equipping readers with the knowledge needed to engage with the concepts presented in this book.

• • • • • • • • • • • • • • • • • • • • • • • • • • • • • • • • • • • • •

# APPENDIX B: DETAILED ETHICAL CASE STUDIES

• • • • • • • • • • • • • • • • • • • • • • • • • • • • •

This appendix provides an in-depth exploration of real-world case studies that illustrate ethical challenges and solutions in AI development and deployment. These case studies serve as practical examples for understanding the importance of ethical considerations and highlight actionable lessons for AI practitioners.

• • • • • • • • • • • • • • • • • • • • • • • • • • • • •

*Case Study 1: Bias in Recruitment AI*

**Scenario**:

A major corporation implemented an AI-powered recruitment tool to streamline hiring processes. The system analyzed resumes and assigned scores based on predicted job performance. However, it was later revealed that the algorithm systematically favored male candidates over female ones.

**Key Issues**:

1. **Bias in Training Data**:

   –     The training data consisted of historical hiring decisions that reflected the organization's past biases.

2. **Lack of Transparency**:

   –     The scoring process was a "black-box," making it difficult to identify and address the source of the bias.

3. **Impact**:

– Qualified candidates were excluded based on gender, violating anti-discrimination laws and ethical hiring practices.

**Actions Taken**:
1. **Bias Detection**:

– The company conducted an audit using tools like IBM's AI Fairness 360 to identify disparities.

2. **Bias Mitigation**:

– Retrained the model with balanced and anonymized data to eliminate gender-specific patterns.

3. **Transparency Improvements**:

– Integrated explainability features to clarify how scores were calculated.

**Lessons Learned**:
• **Importance of Representative Data**: Training data must be diverse and reflective of the population being served.

• **Need for Regular Audits**: Continuous monitoring can detect and address biases before they cause harm.

• **Transparency as a Solution**: Explainability builds trust and aids in identifying issues.

• • • • • • • • • • • • • • • • • • • • • • • • • • • • • • • • • • •

*Case Study 2: Autonomous Vehicle Accident*
**Scenario**:
In 2018, an autonomous vehicle operated by Uber struck and killed a pedestrian in Arizona during a test drive. Investigations revealed multiple failures in the vehicle's AI system.
**Key Issues**:
1. **Failure in Object Recognition**:

– The AI system misclassified the pedestrian as an

inanimate object and failed to take corrective action.

2. **Over-Reliance on Automation**:

- The human safety driver was not actively monitoring the system.

3. **Ethical Oversight**:

- The testing protocols lacked rigorous safety and ethical reviews.

**Actions Taken**:
1. **Revised Safety Protocols**:

- Autonomous vehicle companies updated testing guidelines to include mandatory human intervention protocols.

2. **Enhanced AI Training**:

- Improved object recognition algorithms through extensive testing with diverse real-world scenarios.

3. **Regulatory Reforms**:

- Governments introduced stricter oversight for autonomous vehicle testing.

**Lessons Learned**:

- **Human-in-the-Loop is Essential**: Autonomous systems must always have human oversight in high-stakes scenarios.

- **Rigorous Testing**: Testing under diverse conditions is critical to ensuring safety.

- **Accountability in Deployment**: Clear responsibility must be established for failures in AI systems.

• • • • • • • • • • • • • • • • • • • • • • • • • • • • • • • • •

*Case Study 3: Facial Recognition Misuse*
**Scenario**:
A law enforcement agency deployed a facial recognition system

to identify suspects in criminal investigations. It was later discovered that the system disproportionately misidentified people of color, leading to wrongful detentions.

**Key Issues:**

1. **Algorithmic Bias:**

   – The system was trained on datasets lacking diversity, leading to inaccuracies for non-Caucasian individuals.

2. **Ethical Violations:**

   – The deployment without safeguards violated privacy rights and due process.

3. **Public Backlash:**

   – The misuse of the technology eroded public trust in AI and the authorities using it.

**Actions Taken:**

1. **Suspension of Deployment:**

   – The agency suspended the use of the system until improvements were made.

2. **Bias Audits:**

   – Partnered with external auditors to evaluate and improve the fairness of the algorithm.

3. **Policy Reforms:**

   – Implemented regulations requiring transparency and accountability in the use of facial recognition technology.

**Lessons Learned:**

• **Diverse Training Data:** AI systems must be trained on datasets that represent all demographics fairly.

• **Privacy Considerations:** Clear consent and legal safeguards are essential when using surveillance technologies.

• **Public Engagement:** Building trust requires open dialogue and accountability.

• • • • • • • • • • • • • • • • • • • • • • • • • • • • • • • •

*Case Study 4: AI-Generated Misinformation*

**Scenario**:

During a major election, AI-generated deepfake videos surfaced, depicting political candidates making inflammatory statements. These videos went viral, influencing public opinion and creating widespread misinformation.

**Key Issues**:

1. **Lack of Authenticity Markers**:

   – The videos lacked watermarks or metadata to indicate they were AI-generated.

2. **Amplification by Social Media**:

   – Algorithms prioritized sensational content, spreading the misinformation rapidly.

3. **Ethical Concerns**:

   – The technology's misuse undermined democratic processes and public trust.

**Actions Taken**:

1. **Implementation of Watermarking**:

   – Developers introduced invisible digital watermarks to authenticate AI-generated content.

2. **AI Detection Tools**:

   – Platforms deployed deepfake detection tools to flag and remove manipulated content.

3. **Public Education**:

   – Awareness campaigns educated users about deepfakes and how to identify them.

**Lessons Learned**:

   • **Proactive Safeguards**: Tools for authenticating AI-generated content must be integrated at the development stage.

- **Social Responsibility**: Platforms must prioritize accuracy over engagement in their content algorithms.

- **Public Awareness**: Educating users is crucial to combating misinformation.

• • • • • • • • • • • • • • • • • • • • • • • • • • • • • • • • • • •

*Case Study 5: Environmental Impact of AI*

**Scenario**:

A tech company deployed a machine learning model requiring extensive computational resources, resulting in high energy consumption and significant carbon emissions.

**Key Issues**:

1. **Energy-Intensive Training**:

   – Training the model consumed as much energy as an average household does in a year.

2. **Lack of Sustainability Metrics**:

   – The environmental impact was not considered during development.

3. **Public Scrutiny**:

   – Critics highlighted the disparity between the company's AI innovation and its sustainability commitments.

**Actions Taken**:

1. **Adoption of Green AI Practices**:

   – Optimized model architectures to reduce computational requirements.

   – Transitioned to using renewable energy sources for data centers.

2. **Carbon Offsetting**:

- Invested in carbon offset programs to mitigate the environmental impact.

3. **Transparency in Reporting:**

- Published annual sustainability reports detailing the environmental impact of AI projects.

**Lessons Learned:**

- **Sustainable Design:** AI systems must balance innovation with environmental responsibility.

- **Energy Optimization:** Efficiency should be a priority during model design and training.

- **Accountability:** Transparency builds trust and promotes sustainable practices.

• • • • • • • • • • • • • • • • • • • • • • • • • • • • • • • • • • •

## Conclusion

These case studies highlight the ethical complexities of AI development and deployment. By learning from these examples, organizations can anticipate challenges, implement safeguards, and ensure their AI systems align with societal values and ethical principles. They serve as a reminder that ethical AI is not only about avoiding harm but also about actively contributing to the greater good.

• • • • • • • • • • • • • • • • • • • • • • • • • • • • • • • • • • •

# APPENDIX C: DECLARATION TEMPLATE FOR ETHICAL AI

• • • • • • • • • • • • • • • • • • • • • • • • • • • • • •

*Introduction*

The **Declaration Template for Ethical AI** is a formal document designed to help organizations publicly commit to responsible AI development and deployment. It provides a framework for expressing alignment with ethical principles, transparency in operations, and accountability to stakeholders. This template can be customized to reflect an organization's specific values, goals, and applications of AI.

• • • • • • • • • • • • • • • • • • • • • • • • • • • • • •

# DECLARATION OF ETHICAL AI COMMITMENT

. . . . . . . . . . . . . . . . . . . . . . . . . . . . . . . . . . .

## 1. Introduction and Purpose

This document outlines [Organization Name]'s commitment to developing and deploying Artificial Intelligence (AI) systems responsibly and ethically. As part of our mission, we recognize the transformative potential of AI and our responsibility to ensure that these technologies are used to benefit humanity, uphold fundamental rights, and align with societal values.

. . . . . . . . . . . . . . . . . . . . . . . . . . . . . . . . . . .

## 2. Ethical Principles

We pledge to adhere to the following core principles in all AI-related activities:

1. **Fairness**:

   – We commit to designing AI systems that are free from bias and promote equity across all demographics.

2. **Transparency**:

   – We will ensure that our AI systems are understandable and their decision-making processes explainable.

3. **Accountability**:

   – We accept full responsibility for the outcomes of our AI systems and will address any unintended consequences.

4. **Privacy**:

–       We prioritize the protection of user data, ensuring compliance with all relevant privacy laws and ethical standards.

5. **Safety**:

–       We will design and deploy AI systems that prioritize user safety and minimize potential harm.

6. **Inclusivity**:

–       We will actively work to make AI technologies accessible and beneficial to all, reducing inequalities and fostering global equity.

7. **Sustainability**:

–       We pledge to consider environmental impacts and promote sustainable practices in AI development.

• • • • • • • • • • • • • • • • • • • • • • • • • • • • • • • •

*3. Organizational Commitments*

As part of this declaration, [Organization Name] commits to the following actions:

1. **Establish Ethical Governance**:

–       Appoint an ethics officer or create an ethics committee to oversee AI projects.

–       Regularly review AI systems for ethical compliance.

2. **Engage Stakeholders**:

–       Include diverse voices, including ethicists, end-users, and underrepresented communities, in the development process.

3. **Promote Transparency**:

–       Publish reports on the ethical implications of AI projects.

- Provide users with clear documentation on AI capabilities, limitations, and safeguards.

4. **Adopt Robust Testing and Monitoring**:

- Conduct rigorous testing to ensure AI systems meet safety and fairness standards.

- Continuously monitor deployed systems for unintended consequences and ethical compliance.

5. **Provide Training and Education**:

- Train employees on ethical AI principles and practices.

- Foster a culture of responsibility and accountability within the organization.

6. **Collaborate with Global Initiatives**:

- Support international efforts to develop and enforce ethical AI standards.

- Share best practices and insights with the wider AI community.

• • • • • • • • • • • • • • • • • • • • • • • • • • • • • • • •

*4. Scope of Application*

This declaration applies to all AI systems, tools, and services developed, deployed, or managed by [Organization Name], as well as partnerships and collaborations involving AI technologies.

• • • • • • • • • • • • • • • • • • • • • • • • • • • • • • • •

*5. Review and Updates*

We acknowledge that the ethical landscape of AI is dynamic. [Organization Name] will review and update this declaration annually to reflect evolving standards, technological advancements, and stakeholder feedback.

• • • • • • • • • • • • • • • • • • • • • • • • • • • • • • • •

*6. Acknowledgment and Accountability*

We invite our employees, users, and partners to hold us accountable to these commitments. Concerns or suggestions regarding our ethical practices can be directed to [Contact Information or Ethics Officer Contact].

• • • • • • • • • • • • • • • • • • • • • • • • • • • • • • • • • • •

*7. Signatures*

By signing this declaration, the undersigned affirm their commitment to upholding the principles and actions outlined above.

| Name | Title | Signature | Date |
|------|-------|-----------|------|
|      |       |           |      |
|      |       |           |      |
|      |       |           |      |

• • • • • • • • • • • • • • • • • • • • • • • • • • • • • • • •

# CUSTOMIZATION NOTES

Organizations can tailor this template to suit their specific needs and priorities. Examples of customization include:

- Adding specific ethical commitments relevant to the industry or technology.

- Including additional sections for employee or partner pledges.

- Localizing the declaration to align with regional laws and cultural considerations.

• • • • • • • • • • • • • • • • • • • • • • • • • • • • • • • • • • • •

## Conclusion

The **Declaration Template for Ethical AI** provides a foundation for organizations to formalize their commitment to responsible AI development. By adopting and adapting this template, organizations can foster trust, accountability, and alignment with societal values, setting a positive example for ethical innovation.

• • • • • • • • • • • • • • • • • • • • • • • • • • • • • • • • • • • •

# APPENDIX D: ETHICAL AI TOOLKIT OVERVIEW

......................................................

*Introduction*

The **Ethical AI Toolkit** is a collection of tools, frameworks, methodologies, and resources designed to support organizations in the responsible development, deployment, and monitoring of AI systems. This overview provides a detailed description of the components included in the toolkit, their functions, and how they can be applied in real-world scenarios to promote ethical compliance.

......................................................

# 1. COMPONENTS OF THE ETHICAL AI TOOLKIT

*1.1 Bias Detection and Mitigation Tools*

Tools to identify and address biases in datasets and AI models.

- **AI Fairness 360 (AIF360):**
  - Developer: IBM
  - Features:
    - A library of metrics for assessing bias.
    - Algorithms to mitigate bias pre-processing, in-processing, and post-processing stages.
  - Application: Evaluating fairness in hiring algorithms, credit scoring systems, and more.

- **Fairlearn:**
  - Developer: Microsoft
  - Features:
    - Provides fairness metrics and mitigation algorithms.
    - Includes visualization dashboards for analyzing disparities.
  - Application: Ensuring equitable treatment in AI models for healthcare and education.

• • • • • • • • • • • • • • • • • • • • • • • • • • • • • • • • •

## *1.2 Explainability and Interpretability Tools*

Tools to make AI decision-making processes transparent and understandable.

- **LIME (Local Interpretable Model-Agnostic Explanations):**
  - Developer: Open source
  - Features:
    - Explains individual predictions for any black-box model.
  - Application: Providing transparency in medical diagnoses or legal decision-making systems.

- **SHAP (SHapley Additive exPlanations):**
  - Developer: Open source
  - Features:
    - Assigns importance values to input features influencing model outputs.
  - Application: Enhancing trust in financial decision-making models.

- **What-If Tool:**
  - Developer: Google
  - Features:
    - Interactive tool to explore AI model predictions and assess fairness.
  - Application: Testing the impact of changes in input features on AI predictions.

• • • • • • • • • • • • • • • • • • • • • • • • • • • • • • • • •

## *1.3 Privacy and Security Tools*

Tools to ensure data privacy and secure handling in AI systems.

- **Differential Privacy Library:**

- Developer: Open source
- Features:
  - Implements differential privacy techniques to anonymize data.
- Application: Sharing aggregate insights without compromising individual privacy.

- **Presidio**:
  - Developer: Microsoft
  - Features:
    - Identifies and redacts sensitive information from datasets.
  - Application: Protecting personal data in text analytics and natural language processing.

. . . . . . . . . . . . . . . . . . . . . . . . . . . . . . . . . . . . . . . . . . . .

*1.4 Ethical Impact Assessment Frameworks*
Frameworks to evaluate the societal and ethical impact of AI systems.
- **AI Ethics Impact Assessment Tool**:
  - Developer: Independent research organizations
  - Features:
    - Guides organizations through assessing ethical risks and benefits.
  - Application: Pre-deployment ethical evaluation for large-scale AI systems.
- **Helsinki Ethical AI Framework**:
  - Developer: City of Helsinki
  - Features:
    - Offers a template for documenting AI

development processes transparently.

- Application: Public sector AI deployments in governance and urban planning.

• • • • • • • • • • • • • • • • • • • • • • • • • • • • • • • • • •

## *1.5 Sustainability and Resource Optimization Tools*
Tools to minimize the environmental impact of AI.
- **Green AI Framework**:
  - Developer: Research community
  - Features:
    - Encourages energy-efficient model training and deployment practices.
  - Application: Reducing carbon footprints of large language models.
- **CodeCarbon**:
  - Developer: Open source
  - Features:
    - Tracks and reports the carbon emissions of AI training.
  - Application: Monitoring environmental impact in academic and corporate AI projects.

• • • • • • • • • • • • • • • • • • • • • • • • • • • • • • • • • •

## *1.6 Continuous Monitoring and Auditing Tools*
Tools to ensure ongoing compliance with ethical standards.
- **Model Monitoring Dashboard**:
  - Developer: Open source and enterprise providers
  - Features:
    - Tracks model performance, bias, and fairness in real-time.

- – Application: Monitoring deployed AI systems in high-stakes applications like finance and healthcare.

- **Ethical Audit Framework**:
  - – Developer: Independent organizations
  - – Features:
    - Provides a structured approach for third-party audits of AI systems.
  - – Application: Annual reviews of compliance with ethical AI guidelines.

. . . . . . . . . . . . . . . . . . . . . . . . . . . . . . . . . . . .

## 1.7 Collaboration and Training Platforms

Resources for fostering interdisciplinary collaboration and training in ethical AI.

- **Partnership on AI (PAI)**:
  - – Developer: Consortium of organizations
  - – Features:
    - Brings together industry, academia, and civil society for ethical AI discussions.
  - – Application: Policy recommendations and training for responsible AI development.

- **AI Ethics Online Courses**:
  - – Providers: Platforms like edX, Coursera, and Udemy
  - – Features:
    - Courses on AI ethics, fairness, and societal impact.
  - – Application: Training employees and students in responsible AI practices.

. . . . . . . . . . . . . . . . . . . . . . . . . . . . . . . . . . . .

# 2. INTEGRATING THE TOOLKIT INTO DEVELOPMENT PIPELINES

*2.1 Stage-Wise Integration*

- **Planning**:

  - Use ethical impact assessment tools to evaluate potential risks and benefits.

- **Data Collection and Preparation**:

  - Apply privacy tools to anonymize sensitive data and fairness tools to detect biases.

- **Model Development**:

  - Incorporate bias detection, mitigation, and explainability tools to ensure compliance during training.

- **Deployment**:

  - Use continuous monitoring tools to track system performance and compliance.

- **Post-Deployment**:

  - Conduct regular audits using auditing frameworks and track KPIs for ethical success.

## 2.2 Collaboration and Training

- Encourage interdisciplinary teams to use collaboration platforms for sharing insights.

- Provide employees with access to training programs for practical understanding of ethical AI.

• • • • • • • • • • • • • • • • • • • • • • • • • • • • • • • • • • •

# 3. CASE STUDIES OF TOOLKIT USAGE

*Case Study 1: Ensuring Fairness in Loan Approvals*

- **Problem**: A bank's AI system exhibited bias against certain demographic groups in loan approvals.

- **Solution**:

  - Used **AIF360** to detect and mitigate biases in the dataset.

  - Applied **LIME** to explain decision-making to regulators and customers.

- **Outcome**: Achieved a significant reduction in bias while maintaining accuracy.

*Case Study 2: Reducing Environmental Impact of AI Training*

- **Problem**: A company's AI model training consumed excessive energy, leading to criticism.

- **Solution**:

  - Used **CodeCarbon** to measure and report emissions.

  - Implemented energy-efficient practices recommended by the **Green AI Framework**.

- **Outcome**: Reduced carbon emissions by 30% while maintaining model performance.

• • • • • • • • • • • • • • • • • • • • • • • • • • • • • • • •

# 4. CHECKLIST FOR USING THE ETHICAL AI TOOLKIT

1. **Assess Ethical Risks**:
   - Use ethical impact assessment tools during project initiation.

2. **Mitigate Bias**:
   - Apply bias detection and mitigation tools to datasets and models.

3. **Ensure Transparency**:
   - Integrate explainability tools like SHAP or LIME into AI systems.

4. **Protect Privacy**:
   - Use privacy tools to anonymize sensitive data and secure user information.

5. **Monitor Continuously**:
   - Deploy monitoring dashboards to track fairness, accuracy, and compliance.

6. **Engage Stakeholders**:
   - Collaborate with ethicists, developers, and users to refine systems.

7. **Promote Sustainability**:

- Adopt green AI practices and track environmental impact.

· · · · · · · · · · · · · · · · · · · · · · · · · · · · · · · · · · ·

## Conclusion

The **Ethical AI Toolkit** equips organizations with the resources needed to design, deploy, and monitor AI systems responsibly. By integrating these tools into development workflows and fostering a culture of accountability, organizations can align their AI initiatives with ethical principles and societal values.

· · · · · · · · · · · · · · · · · · · · · · · · · · · · · · · · · · ·

www.ingramcontent.com/pod-product-compliance
Lightning Source LLC
Chambersburg PA
CBHW071456220526
45472CB00003B/826